The Monologue Bin: Original Monologues For Teens and Adults

by

Jim Chevallier

PERMISSIONS, ROYALTIES AND MODIFICATIONS

Published by:

Chez Jim
P.O. Box 103
North Hollywood, CA 91603

☐ *These monologues have been road-tested by the Den.* ☐

Table of Contents

NOTE: Age ranges and gender are indicated for convenience. However many pieces here are appropriate for multiple types.

Introductory notes

Age ranges and gender

Few monologues are so specific that they can't be used by actors of different ages and types, and a number of actors have suggested I eliminate these categories entirely. But some readers will need them if they are in a hurry.

In a word: use them, but don't be limited by them.

If you've never studied...

You should. It's fun. It's useful.

Until you do, though, here's two quick hints on how to approach monologues:

- Choose a *specific* person to talk to.
- Decide *specifically* what you want from them.

Try addressing different people. Try picking different objectives. If you've never done this, you'll be amazed how much the same monologue can change. (As the author, let me assure you: there is no 'right' way to do these monologues. They are tools for you to use as you need.)

Otherwise, two books that many experienced actors recommend are Uta Hagen's *A Challenge for the Actor* and Michael Shurtleff's *Audition*. There's lots of other classics out there, but these two are especially concrete and to the point.

Finally, whatever else you do, always, always have **fun**.

Jim Chevallier

TEEN: Female

Sister Santa

Ho, ho, ho!

I am too Santa Claus, kid. Yeah, I'm a girl. Like duh-uh. – Because I need the money, OK? It's either you little germ-donors or cooking Christmas burgers at the local take-out.

Hey, but enough about me. What greedy little totally unreasonable demand do you want to make of the Great White Beard? – No, I didn't grow the beard. I'm a girl, OK? We don't as a general thing grow beards. Hey, look, would you rather have me or some red-eyed wino who's working off his last bottle of rotgut? Like liquor breath, do you? Well, then, work with me here, OK? I got midterms next week, plus a female problem you do not want to know about. So trust me, I am not in the mood.

What'll it be then? A molded plastic semi-automatic so you can imitate your favorite mad gunman? Some bloodthirsty boy-doll that crawls around on its belly, armed to the teeth? A little remote control tank you can send shooting through pedestrians' feet and scare the Pampers off frail old ladies? Come on, sweetie, you just tell Sister Santa here what violence and mayhem disguised as a toy will put your little testosterone-tainted heart all a flutter. Rat-a-tat-tat! Boom, boom, boom!

No, I do NOT have a problem with men! Where do you get this stuff? What kind of shows do your parents let you watch, anyway? And no, there is nothing weird about a female Santa! You better get used to it kid, when you grow up, there's going to be girls EVERYWHERE. Yeah, that's right, we're even in the army!

Ah no, now I've gone and made you cry. Hey, can we get a nurturer over here? Anyone into being maternal?

Geez....

Tracy And The Formerly Young Hopeful

Hi. Come in. Have a seat. Would you like anything? Mineral water, fruit juice? Sorry. No beer. I'm underage.

Well, now – Excuse me? My boss? I'm sorry. I should have made that clear. I am the boss. That's right. Big League Talent. That's me. I own the place.

Well, yes, I am a little young. Not that young. – Uh, no, I don't mind. I'm sixteen. And a few months. Yourself?

Thirty five? Excuse me. I don't mean to be rude, but are you sure? To tell the truth, you look a little older. And then you know so many people are afraid to admit they're over forty. But let me be perfectly clear: this business is about talent. Age has nothing to do with it. Really. Let me tell you, when I was acting –   Oh, not anymore. I retired. At thirteen. I started when I was three. Oh yeah. I've done tons of films. A little Broadway. But what can I say? It gets boring after a while.

Wait, wait, don't get me wrong. I'm not saying being an actor is boring. I mean, I'm sure you had fun playing... Uh what does it say here? "Crushed guy" in *Jurassic Park*? Gee I saw that movie. Which crushed guy were you? Oh they cut it out. Gee, isn't that terrible? First "Schpluch!", then "Snip!". – Just joking.

So, anyway, I figured who makes more money, actors or agents? School wasn't a problem. I was already doing home schooling, you know, what with being in all those movies.

Uh, excuse me, are you all right? You look a little pale. – Anyway, like I said a lot of people think this business has been completely taken over by young people, But let me tell you, that's a complete myth.

Damn! Look at the time, I'm already late for my next appointment. Hey, look, thanks for coming in. I'm sure you'll find someone to represent you. But the truth is, I've already got someone in your age range. Really. It's true. He's almost thirty.

Oh yeah, there's room for everybody out there. It's wide open.

Kissless Nick

OK, so here's my problem. My name is Nick, I'm a girl and I am 14. And I like guys who don't even know I exist.

People often say, "Nick, you scare me," and I say, "Thank you!", 'cause people that are different make the world interesting. But guys don't always get it. They don't.

I did sort of go out with this boy that I really liked, but we broke up the first month because all his friends were teasing and annoying. Plus, the day after our first date, I got my period. It was really weird. So I got these major butterflies in my stomach when I saw him. I must have acted really queer.

The whole time I wanted to kiss him. French kiss. Even though I've never kissed anyone. Peck or French. But I figured once you start, it doesn't matter which you do. Anyway, my friend says it's really easy to French. All you do is have your mouth open when you kiss and if the other person's mouth is open too, just slide in the tongue.

On top of which he had braces. So I'm like, should I kiss him anyway, even though he has braces?

So now it's too late. I should have just gone for it, I guess. But now he's going out with some hoochie. You see them together, and they're like Frenching, all the time. So I feel like a complete moron. Which I am.

I haven't even been out on a date since that except once on a sympathy date with one of my friends' brothers. But he was really a big loser, so I didn't have any fun. And no way was I letting him kiss me. Peck or French.

Well that's my problem. But the way I figure, it's got to happen, doesn't it? I can't be single and kissless for my whole life.

Can I?

S-word

What did you call me?

No, no, wait. Don't walk away. You've got quite the mouth there. It was sure working fine a minute ago. Why stop now? Don't be shy.

Let me help you: S... L... U... Coming back to you now, is it?

So, I've been out with more than one guy. Wow. Imagine that. You know what? You bet I have. Boys like me, if you want to know. And if they're halfway decent to me, I like them too.

This, lest you miss the point, would not include you.

You'd love to get with lots of girls, wouldn't you? You'd love to have a little list of your own. You'd be quite the rooster then, wouldn't you? You'd be quite the cockle-doodle-doo.

As it is, you can shorten that by about four syllables. You can do that, right? I'll bet you know all about short things.

But let me be a little popular, let me profit from what are, by the way, quite considerable opportunities, – quite sizeable, you might say – and you, Mr. Moral Oral, call me a – What was that word? Want to say it again?

What's the matter? Cat got your tongue?

Look, since it's a safe bet you're not going anywhere tonight, why don't you stop by the science lab and see if you can borrow a microscope? That way when you go home tonight, you won't have to spend hours looking for your little playmate before you put him in a chokehold.

Me, I'll be busy. Would you believe? I've got a date.

Fake ID

The worst thing is, $50 is cheap. Not for me, no. If my brother-in-law hadn't felt sorry for me, I wouldn't even have come up with that. But I did. Not a penny more, but at least I got the fifty bucks. Which is pretty much bottom of the line. Nowhere near what the pros charge.

The worst part after that is going downtown. There's this street everybody knows about where these guys hang around, and you walk by them, real close, without looking at them, and they whisper "Need ID? Need ID?", and then you pick one, or you look for the guy your friends told you about, and you give him your picture. And the money. That's right. You have to pay them up front. And yeah, sometimes they rip you off. That's why you have to know who to go to. Then you wait, have coffee or something, and then they come back, and you have it. You have your fake ID.

OK, that's scary enough, getting the money and then hoping this guy with gold chains and lots of tattoos but no teeth doesn't rip you off. But then, you figure, you're home free. You can hang out with the big girls now. You can party one hundred percent.

Only, I went out with my friends that night to the Sludge, and it was going to be my big night. I have been dying to go to that place. So I hand my ID to the bouncer – this guy was huge, I had to bend my head back to talk to him – and he takes my ID, and he looks at it, and he LAUGHS. And he hands it to this other guy leaning against the wall. And HE laughs. Then the first guy, the bouncer, hands it back to me and he says, "Oh honey, get your money back. You so got ripped off. You got ripped off big time." Then he laughs again, and starts letting the other people through. And I'm just standing there, with everybody looking at me as they're walking in.

Oh my God, I was so embarrassed. I was mortified. Now I'll never get into the Sludge. Not for another two years anyway. And on top of that, I'm out fifty bucks.

Life can't get any worse than this. Can it?

Queen of Steel

You know who I want to be like? Stalina, Queen of Steel.
Swish! Whap! Gnah!

That's how she fights. She thrusts, she pounces, she clangs; she clicks, she feints, she flies. She lunges forward, she shifts to the right; she closes in, she springs back.

And she always wins! That's what's so cool! You always know, no matter how bad a scrape she's in, no matter how far she's outnumbered, even if she's sick or wounded or just so down she's about to give up, you just know she's gonna win.

And not just because she's the heroine. Not just because, OK, it's her show. But because she's like that! Because she's got the stuff. You know, the grits, the goods, the guts. She always wins because she KNOWS she's supposed to win. That's what you can always tell. It doesn't matter how much she looks like she wants to give up, how even all her friends have let her down, how everything, absolutely everything is going wrong… Deep down inside, no matter what the situation, no matter what the odds, she KNOWS she's supposed to win.

And that, that's how I want to feel. Just, like, all the time.Like I'm *supposed* to win!

Getting Ahead

Who needs school? I met this guy, he's a photographer. He says I can be a model. He's gonna have me over to his studio to do some test shots, and then he's gonna take them down to New York, and then he says I should have no trouble getting discovered. Right away. Because they're always looking for people with interesting looks and he says I've got a really interesting look.

And then they send you to Paris. After they discover you. So you can work on your book. Only you have to be careful, he says, because some of those French guys, they're real sleazebags. But he says I should be OK. Because I've got a good head on my shoulders. That's what he says. A good head.

And after you're in Paris, you do the cover of *Vogue*. Because that's what makes you famous. They don't pay too well, which sucks, but you have to do it. Sometimes you have to sacrifice, you know? To get ahead. And after that when you come back to New York, you're a big deal. Though some girls, I guess they don't come back. They marry counts and playboys and people like that. But me, I'd come back. 'Cause I'm not like that, you know? It's like he says. I've got a good head.

Anyway, that's when you open a restaurant, and get your own TV show, and become a spokes model. All that. All the real model stuff.

But that's later. You have to take it one step at a time. Because it's not like it happens all at once.

I mean, you have to be realistic.

Sole Mate

He is so HOT. I don't care if they do say he's a... you know. They just say that 'cause he's so pretty. Like, just because guys like you, you have to like them. I don't think so.

You know who he likes? Really? Promise you won't tell anyone? 'Cause people can get weird about this stuff. Super strange. – OK. You're not going to believe this.

He... likes... ME. Really! Totally! I'm his dream girl. OK, so he's never met me. No problem. What it is, is, he's got this ideal woman. I know. I read it in *Teen Confidential*. He wants a girl who's got a really good heart, and a head on her shoulders, and can stand on her own two feet. I can do that, right? And another thing. She can't like him just because he's a star. She has to like him for him-SELF. Well, I do. I totally do. It's like he was in... you know... the big one. When he's poor, you know, and the other one, you know the fat one, she's got all this money? Well, you see that doesn't matter, the fact that he's poor. I mean, I don't care. Because I love him for his soul. For who he really is. Not like her. I mean, she just loves him because he's in the movie, so she has to.

So it doesn't matter that he hasn't met me, because he already knows who I am. In his mind. It's just like, I have to meet him, you know? That's the problem. It's not like I'm not doing my part. I keep writing him all these letters. But he's not getting them. I know, because he hasn't called. I sent my picture, and my e-mail, and my cell phone number. But nothing so far. Zilch. It's really unfair, you know? That they're not giving him my letters. Because I'm a nobody, you know, to them, and he's like a prince. He's poor, but at the same time, he's a prince. And they don't want him to be with a nobody. Even if she's the right one. So that's why. That's why they're not giving him my letters.

And it's just not fair. It's just, like, really, really unfair.

Mom Babe

Please don't wear that dress. It makes you look like… well, a mom.

Guys don't want to date their moms. Not even guys your age. Especially not guys your age. They want to date babes. Even chicks your age. They want you to be babes.

Now, I know you're my mom and all, and I probably shouldn't be saying this, but you totally have it in you to be the ultimate babe. This I believe. This I swear.

But not in that dress. That dress is the anti-babe. That dress is babe-icide. It's like a great big sign saying, "Keep your eyes on the hairdo, pal! Nothing to see down here. Down here is off-limits. Visits not encouraged. Intruders keep out."

From a strict marketing point of view, is this the message you wish to convey? I think not.

Do not hide the honey from the bear. Do not hide the apple from the worm. Do not hide the blossom from the bee.

Put on something sultry, something clinging, something that shows what you've got. Then dab a little color on those cheeks and go forth in all your glory, go forth in all your babe glory and conquer as is your due. Oh you babe you, oh sweet beloved mom-babe of mine.

Before the News

I was so sleepy. Our school was closed that day, so I didn't have to wake up. And he didn't want to wake me up, not all the way. Just enough to kiss him goodbye, like I did everyday. He smelled all clean, like shaving lotion and toothpaste. And he kissed me on the cheek and I felt my own skull as he stroked my hair. "Love you, pigeon." He always said that. And I tried to make cooing sounds like I did when I was awake, but instead it came out like a little grunt. Still, I kissed his cheek when he put it against my lips, and I took his hand – his big, strong hand – between mine.

Then he got up, and he walked out, and I fell asleep. I must have fallen asleep for a long time. I dreamed of people in color, like cartoons, in a world that was all beige and white and pale yellow and light blue. And sometimes in this world I could fly. He was there, and he threw me in the air like he did when I was small, only this time I kept going up, up and up, waving to him and then to the neighbors and then to the whole town. And then they all disappeared and I was flying, flying by a tower, the tower where he worked, right outside the windows way up at the top. And then I stopped, and I began to fall. I began to fall back down, faster and faster. And someone was calling me, far below.

I woke, and it was my mother, calling to me from downstairs, calling for me to hurry, to hurry up and come down, and see the news on the TV.

Johnson's Surprise

How do I look? Pretty lousy, huh? Take a good look. Because I'm just gonna get worse. I don't expect to be looking better for a good long time.

Be sure to write that in your report. Be sure to tell them that. OK, and if you get a chance, ask them. Ask them why they did it. Because it's the law? Then ask them why the laws are so stupid.

She didn't want me. She still doesn't. Why'd she go to so much trouble to get me back? After all those years? Why did they let her take me away from Eva?

Do you know, Eva's house was cold in the winter, and you couldn't walk anywhere, and sometimes the pipes froze. And she couldn't cook either. Not even Swedish meatballs. All she could make was this one dish. It was from Sweden too. Johnson's Surprise. All it was was sliced potatoes with lots and lots of cream, and herring. I don't even like herring. But when it was cold, she'd make that, and after it came out of the oven, we'd sit in the kitchen, spooning it out of the casserole, just the two of us together. The two of us and our Johnson's Surprise.

That's what I remember most about Eva. That and how she cried when they took me away.

And now we live in this dirty apartment where the pipes bang, and we can hear the neighbors fight, and if I want anything to eat, I have to go buy it and then make it myself. Though she does give me the food stamps. When she's there. Half the time she isn't.

But it doesn't matter, because I'm not there much either now. In fact, I'm there less and less. But I'll bet you can tell by looking at me, I'm finding lots of things to do. Lots.

So you tell them that when you see them, tell them how it all worked out, and then you ask them again, why? Why was this the right thing to do? Because there's only one thing I ever wanted, and Eva gave me lots of it, lots of that, and that damned Johnson's Surprise.

The Weird Kid

I guess people think we're a lot alike. The popular kids. King and queen of the hallway. Hey, a lot of people even think we should go out. You included, right?

Wasn't that what you were trying to do? Impress me? By ragging that kid in front of everybody? What the hell, he's the weird kid, right? Nobody likes him. Gonna give somebody a hard time, that's the one, yessiree. And you really got to him. Oh yeah. He was upset. 'Cause you're good. You really know how to hit your mark.

Now here's the thing. You don't remember me, do you? Before the last year or so. It's like I just moved here. It's like I came out of nowhere.

Except I didn't. I was always here. Only I was invisible. Not just to you. To everybody. Bad hair, glasses, no social skills. Did not play well with others. Smart – did you know I have a really high I.Q.? –, but not someone you'd notice unless you stepped on them. And then you'd get annoyed they were in your way.

This was not fun. I was not enjoying this. So I changed.

Amazing what a haircut can do, huh? And contacts. The right clothes. Oh, and puberty. I can't take credit for puberty. But I sure take credit for all the rest. Because I didn't start out popular. I worked at it. I worked at it hard.

Pretty good job, huh? Don't try to tell me *you're* not impressed. Girls talk, you know. Word gets back.

Only, I wouldn't get your hopes up. Not after what you did to that kid. He may never be popular. Hell, who knows if he wants to be? But one thing you can count on. No matter how far outside he stays, no matter deep I get into every inner circle, no matter how many people ignore him and can't get enough of me, I'll always be able to see things a little his way. I'll always understand how he feels.

And tell me, just now, how do you think he feels about you?

Report Card

OK, here's the problem. You know my dad? Well, he's not really my dad. My mom married him when I was six. But he says he is. "You're my daughter," he says, "Just like you were mine. You know that, don't you?" And I guess I do. I guess he is my dad. Not just because he says he is. But because he wants to be.

But, OK, here's the thing. He wants me to do well in school. He says it's really important. Otherwise, he says, I'll end up like him. Working all the time and never making any money. That's the only thing he ever gets mad about is my grades. Because he says, that's my future, and if my grades go down, it's like my future goes right down with them.

Only, I don't know why, I just can't care about school. Even with all my friends here, I just want to be somewhere else. And when I go home, I can't go anywhere until I finish my homework. Which I almost never do. So I don't get to watch TV, or go out, or anything.

Which just makes me hate school even more.

So, OK, we got our report cards and I know you did really well, like you always do.

But here's the thing. Mine sucks. My dad's gonna be so angry when he sees it. Or maybe not. Maybe he'll just be sad.

That's even worse. When he's just really quiet.

So anyway, remember how you copied my signature that time, just for fun?

Here's the check my dad signed for my locker rental. I copied it before I gave it in. That was smart, huh?

Can you just copy his signature a few times, you know, to get it right? And then, could you sign it here, on my report card?

Please? 'Cause I just can't let him see it. I can't.

Anesthesia

When Daddy died, I had to be strong. For my brother. He was only nine, and I was almost twelve. So I could handle it a lot better. Sure, it was a shock. He just suddenly got sick. It turned out he'd had cancer for a while, but they didn't find it until just before he died.

Sure, I cried some. It's not like I didn't feel anything. But mostly I was worried about Albie. He didn't understand at all, and sometimes he'd cry, for hours, but sometimes he'd just get angry, like it wasn't fair and me and Mom were supposed to stop it. And I'd try to explain, but he didn't want to hear it. He didn't want to hear about cancer, and how it sometimes just happened. He would explode and start to scream, like if he screamed hard enough it would bring Dad back.

And I couldn't do anything, except watch. Because he wouldn't even let me touch him. But then, other times, he wouldn't say anything at all. He'd just come up to me while I was studying or watching TV, and he'd crawl up against me, and hug me, not saying a word.

Mom needed help too. Because there were all the bills, and now she had to work extra hours. So I'd fix Albie dinner, and I'd clean the house, and do all those things she didn't have time to do anymore.

With all that, you know, I didn't have much time to think about Dad, or to be sad or anything. 'Cause I was always so busy, and always so worried about Albie, and about Mom too. I didn't have time to be worried about my own feelings. I just didn't have time.

I guess that's a good thing, huh?

Jasmine

Jasmine's what I smell when I feel sad. It doesn't matter where – at the mall, in the locker room, on the way home. What's around me might be gas fumes, sweat, cigarettes. Suddenly through it all I'll smell this sweet delicate scent, the slight, sure hint of a white flower. A flower I've hardly ever seen. Or smelled. And never at those moments. Never when I'm down. But right along with the sting of whatever caused the pain – a teacher snapping at me, a friend not saying "hi", my boyfriend looking at someone else – wherever it comes from – being put down, being ignored, or just being, sometimes, just thinking everything's awful, and I want to be left alone – it can cut at me, it can suffocate me, it can make me feel like there's no light at all – and yet, while it's rushing through me, this hurt, this failure, this hopelessness that just takes me over at times – I'll smell it, smell the jasmine, secret and shy, and in the middle of these moments when I feel like nothing at all, when I feel like I'm slipping and about to go under, there's a sweetness, a kindness, a soft white flower that whispers my name, that whispers to me and won't let me go.

TEEN: Male

Pie

The whole time I was cooking, she looked preoccupied. Not that I noticed. I was totally into making my pie.

She offered to help cut the apples, but I said, "No, no. I want to do everything myself." And I did. Just rolling the dough and dusting it with flour made me feel like quite the master chef. And then, when I took out this nice brown pie, all crisp around the edges and glazed on top, let me tell you, that was a good moment. She watched me put it down. My first pie! It was still pretty hot, so I said, "We'd better let it cool off." So we sat there, with the smell of the crust and the apples and cinnamon coming up from the pie between us. She smiled, a proud smile, maybe because I was such a good cook. I don't know. Hey, I was pretty proud of it. That smell alone... Not to mention that a year before that, I would have been too stoned to boil water, never mind make my own pie.

Then she reached out and put her hand on my wrist. I could feel her heart beating. "What?" I said. She looked at me and took a deep breath. And that's when she told me. "You're right," she said. "You haven't actually asked me yet, but I think you already know: Jace isn't your father."

Lion

Whoa! You gotta hear this. You won't believe it.

After we won the wrestling championship, we all went out to party. Everybody was buying me drinks and telling me how great I was. And I have to admit, I was pretty proud of myself. That other guy was big. A real goon. But I beat him. I beat him good.

Only, you know what? That was nothing. Listen to this.

I woke up pretty shaky the next day, and I figured I'd clear my head. Go for a hike. So I drove out to the mountains and I took a nice long walk, way up into the woods and beyond. I got up to some rocks where you could see the valley way below. It was beautiful. Peaceful, quiet. Fabulous view. So I started walking slowly, looking out at the valley, lost in my own thoughts – and walked right into a mountain lion.

For real. Fur, fangs, claws. The works. And wicked bad breath. Which I can tell you because he was on me, like that! Up close and personal. The mutt was trying to take me down.

I guess I should have been scared. But you know how I wrestle my neighbor's shepherd? That was how this felt. Only harder. Because Kitty was way way stronger than Fido. Still, claws, teeth? Done that. I knew to push my elbows into his arms so he couldn't slash me. And then I dug my thumbs into his windpipe. Oh, it didn't kill him. No need to call the rangers on me. In fact, it barely slowed him down. That animal could fight. But so could I. And for like two minutes, we're there, right up against each other, pushing and panting away. Breath to breath, eye to eye.

Then, all of sudden, he breaks loose. And off he goes, just like that. Out of sight.

Let me tell you. I stood up with the stink of that animal on me and the mountains all around, and the valley far below, and I felt good, my friend. I felt gigantic.

Because, I'm here to tell you, *that* was a bout. *That* was a championship.

Poem

Honestly, I don't know how it happened. I was waiting for my ride, and someone had left this book on the bench. Hart Crane. Funny name, huh? But I opened it up, and I just started reading. And – how about this? – I liked it. In fact, I took the book with me. I'm a little embarrassed about that. Probably the person forgot it there and came back looking for it later. But that's what I did. I took it with me. And now I read it every night. Between practice and going out.

Only, what's happening now is, I start getting antsy for practice to end. And I'm starting to show up late for dates. Which some guys do on purpose. But not me. I'm not like that.

What I'm trying to say is, I'm changing. It's like I'm becoming this other creature, a creature I never even knew existed, and yet, it's me. Almost as if I was all fur and paws before, and now all of a sudden I'm growing wings.

Now do you understand? That's why. That's why I'm a little different lately. And it's scary. Because I feel like I'm about to lose all my friends. I overheard someone in the locker room say I was acting a little strange. And that just made me feel, well, dizzy. Because I realized, I could end up being pretty lonely.

What I'm saying is, would you read one? Just one. Just try. It won't hurt you. I promise. Only, it might change you a little.

What the hell. Give it a try.

Just one.

Someone's at the Door

Hi. I'm your kid.

Oh, don't look so damn surprised. You knew I'd show up one day. Didn't you? You must have at least considered it. This kind of thing happens all the time. Especially now, what with the Internet and all.

So, what do you think? I look like something you wished you'd raised? Me, I'm pretty pleased. I think I came out OK.

We do kind of look alike, don't we? Wow. That's a rush. I've never seen anyone I was related to before. Not by blood, anyway.

We're not half-bad, are we? In the family. Hey, I'm complimenting you here. And myself too. For sure. But still.

Look, you don't have to invite me in or anything. You may have noticed, I'm kind of on the independent side. I just wanted to get a quick look, you know. Kind of check out the gene pool. So, now that I've done that…

Come in? You're inviting me in? Well, OK, if you're…

I mean, sure, I've got time. Well, you know, a little.

Lead the way.

Dad.

Foot Fire

Dance? Can I dance?

One thing I can do is DANCE. Yes! I can split and spill and spin like a hurricane in a hurry. I can waltz and rock and hop and tango. I can bust moves and dig the groove. I can heat my feet so sweet they'll scorch the boards and singe your socks right through your shoes. I can dip and lead and leap and kneel, I can preach the rhythm and speak the beat, I can take your toes to Heaven and lead your legs to the Promised Land. I can make you weep with wonder and shimmy with joy!

I am that good, I am that fine. I am the sultan, I am the king, I am lightning on a leash, I am an earthquake from my hips on down! I can high-five your heartbeat and syncopate it silly, I can pick up your pulse and teach it to fly.

I may seem sleepy, I may look lonesome, I may get my name mixed up with my sign. But get me out on that dance floor, turn up the tunes and take down the lights – I'll show you the shine of my wings, I'll show you the shape of my shift and glide.

Come to me slowly, come to me sad. I'm the one who can fool that feeling, I'm the one who can switch those gears. Because the one thing I can do is mate with the music, the one thing I can do is DANCE.

Besides the Points

She's got – Well, that's not important. There's more to girls than – still, she really does have nice... but don't get me wrong. She's smart, really smart. And I'm not just saying that. I don't even really notice her... Well, at least, it's not like it's all I think about. She gets good grades, I know that. Kind of a brain actually. Not that that scares me. Hell no. I can handle strong women. I think. To tell the truth, I haven't had that much experience. But I think I could handle them...Uh-huh...

OK. Really. Come on, girls are girls, people, right, just like guys. People with... Well, OK, it's not like we're exactly alike. You have to have some differences. But that's no reason we can't talk, you know, like real people? You know like with guys, just a normal conversation? It's not like I'm going to keep staring at her... Well they are kind of...

I dunno, what's considered a normal size? Academically speaking?

So anyway, what do you think? Should I ask her out?

Gimme That

Gimme that. Come on. Don't be a dweeb.

You totally are. Oh totally. Mr. Don't-You-Dare-It's-Mine. Like a little girl. You'd think I was trying to take your right arm.

You know you can get another one. Yes you can. You totally can. Oh, for sure.

You just don't want me to have it. That is so lame. You just can't stand that I could be like a little bit as lucky as you are. Right? That's it, isn't it? You want to be the Man. You want everybody else to just look at you, tongues hanging out, drool dripping, all huffing and puffing like a hound dog, because they would so like to have what you've got, what you've got right there, even though you could get twenty more like that, oh no, you could have a hundred and damn you would just put the mothers under lock and key, man you'd go out and get yourself a friggin' vault, just so you could keep them and nobody else would get any.

Oh you would. You so totally would.

That is sad, man. Let me tell you, that is lame.

C'mon, let me hold it. Just for a minute?

High Dive

You want me to jump off that? Just, like, ker-boing, straight up and straight down?

You're serious about this now?

I know lots of kids do it. I've seen them. Do it all the time.

But other kids do all sorts of things. Smoke. Did you know smoking's bad for you? Oh yeah. Terrible. But there they are, puffing away.

How about drag racing? See that article last week? Cops busted a whole group, and that was after warning them. But they knew it was dangerous. That's why they did it. Some kids just love doing dangerous stuff.

That would not be me.

I think the human survival instinct is a thing of beauty. An aesthetic marvel.

Jumping off high places, on the other hand, I find conceptually unappealing. Maybe it's the image of that SNAP! as you break your neck. Lacks symmetry somehow.

Very rare, you say? Hardly ever happens?

Well, sure. But look at the lotto. What are the chances against winning that? And yet people do. Happens all the time.

I'm just saying.

You really want me to do this, huh?

OK, OK.

Don't rush me.

Any minute now.

Movie Hell

Oh dude, I love this actor! – Don't worry, they can't hear us. – Do you remember when he was in... Why's that guy turning around? – Oh. Don't worry about it. – But someone said he's not so good in this...

Oh! Look! Look! – Huh? Oh, OK, I'm sorry. But did you see that? You didn't? Oh, I'm sorry. Yeah, yeah, I'll try not to distract you. I'll shut up.

.....

Unh... Ah... Oh my God. Uh-oh. Oh man, I know what's gonna happen... Oh, right. Sorry.

....

Wow! Oh man! That was so... OK, OK, but did you see that? Did you? – Yeah. Well, yeah, it is right up there on the screen.

Oh for Godssakes, what is this guy's problem? He should chill, right? It's not like he can hear what we're saying. – Yeah, well, "we", I meant me. Sure. It's just an expression.

Damn, he's doing it again. Come on, dorkface, turn around and watch the damn film.

Look, I'm sorry, but that's just plain obnoxious. Isn't it?

Jesus, you go to watch a film, you just want to have a little fun and some moron ruins it for you. I'm sorry, but that's just plain inconsiderate.

Oh, look, look! Oh man, I love this guy!

Groaning Up

What's so great about growing up?

The way it looks to me, everything slows way down. It's like they put you in this harness and then they make you pull and the next thing you know you're an ox: big and heavy and slow. And dull. That's the worst part. You look at people over thirty and you know exactly how they're going to be. They've got their job and they've got their ideas and maybe they're married and so they've got that too, and they just get into their groove and they start walking it, you know, they just keep going round and round until it becomes this rut, and after a while it gets so deep that the best they can do is not sink in it, sink until they disappear.

So what I'm saying is, what's the point? Why would you want to end up like that, when you can be young and take chances and have ideas? You know, while you still can be somebody? Have a life. Why would you want to do that, huh? Why would you want to just, like, give up?

It's not like you don't have a choice.

Devotion

After your dad tried to have me arrested on our first date, and your ex-boy friend skipped karate practice to tell me to keep away from you, and your girlfriend spread rumors that I'd hired a hypnotist to get you to go out with me, and after that graffiti that said my boyfriend would be jealous if I kept seeing you, and after that cartoon in the school paper showing you in the clutches of a giant jellyfish that looked a lot like me, not to mention the car troubles I've had since we started dating, and the funny taste my food had just before I got sick, and those fire ants I found in my sheets, and the letters I've been getting with cut-out words and the e-mail that wiped out my hard drive after showing me your picture with a big red circle with a bar across it - Well, of COURSE, I still want to see you.

Why ever would you think I wouldn't?

Mix-up

Don't tell me these are my real parents. With those clothes? And working actual jobs? Normal jobs? Do you see me in an office every day? Or out selling stuff? Oh, I'll make money for sure. Millions. But for my talent. Not at any nine to five.

And the music they listen to. I've had anesthesia that was more exciting. Please. And they keep telling me to turn mine down. Because it makes the walls shake. It's supposed to make the walls shake. That's what makes it so cool.

Mostly, it's that they don't understand me. At all. We don't speak the same language. It's like we're at the U. N., shouting across that big assembly hall, only without any translators. And they're talking about diamond mines and the price of oil, and I'm talking about indigenous peoples and world peace.

No wonder we can't agree.

No, it's taken me a long time, but now I know it. For sure. These are NOT my parents. There's been an awful mistake.

First thing next week, I'm calling that hospital

The Art of Normal

Why do people have to be different? I don't like that.

Don't tell me they can't help it. They could if they wanted to. It's not that hard to be normal.

It's not like I want to hurt them or anything. I just don't want them around me.

'Cause I'm alright. I'm OK. And if people see me with them, they might think I'm not, you know? That I'm like them.

And I'm not. At least, I try not to be. I try to be normal. Supernormal. More normal than normal. It's not that hard, you know, if you work at it. You can dress like other people. You can listen to what they say. And then make sure you're saying the same thing. Or something close. It can't be exactly the same. 'Cause people think that's weird too.

It's hard if you're too fat or too skinny. Or short. Or too tall. It's hard to change that. But you can try. You do whatever it takes: diet, eat a lot, wear platforms, hunch. Depending. Whatever it takes to fit in.

Sure, it's a lot of work. And you've got to watch it all the time. You have to be extra careful. Or else someone might notice. That you're different.

And you don't want that. You don't want them to notice that. Or, if you do, keep away from me, OK?

Please?

'Cause I really don't want to attract any attention.

OK?.

First

It's not like I came on to her. I'm not real good at that stuff. Also, she wasn't ugly or anything. But I wasn't thinking about her that way.

We talked some, and I asked did she need anything, and she said, "Well, you could rub my back." That didn't seem like a big deal. So she took off her t-shirt and her jeans and I started to rub her back. After a while she was making all these happy sounds, and then she pulled me down and we started kissing. But that's all. All I did anyway. Finally she said, "Have you ever done this?" What else could I say? No. Which felt a little stupid. Because it seemed like everybody around me already had.

After that, she took over, and told me how to touch her and all. And she was really careful, but it was like she was laughing a little the whole time. And then finally she pulled me on top of her and tugged a little and that was it.

I wasn't a virgin anymore.

She smelled nice actually. Cleaner than she looked. And it felt good, when we started. Not as good as I thought it would, but pretty good anyway. And we did it once more, and then we fell asleep. And then again this morning before she left.

So that's why I'm so tired. I'm sorry.

What I wanted to ask you, though, is it always like that? Just OK?

Cause somehow I just thought it would be more special.

Suffering

What I really, really want to do is hurt something. An animal, for instance. A cat or a puppy. Something big enough to really feel it, but too small to fight back. And that'd make a lot of noise: yapping, screeching; frantic, desperate, pitiful cries. So that anyone hearing it would feel sorry. Or maybe just get upset and wish it would stop.

Because people don't really care if someone else suffers, not most of them. But if you really disturb them, if you make it harder for them to concentrate on their chocolate bar or their romance novel or on pictures of their girlfriend all tied up and loving it, well, if you make it so it's hard to keep their face down, with their mouth wrapped around whatever it is they're trying to taste, to suck the essence out of, well then, they won't like it, in fact they'll get very mad at you, and think you're a terrible person, and get up all outraged and all, and say, "Hey you, what are you doing to that poor helpless creature? Can't you see it's SUFFERING?"

Which at least would be something, wouldn't it? For them to at least notice that?

YOUNGER ADULT: Female

Stupenda

Please don't tell me you stood in line. Honey, girls who are just OK stand in line. Girls who may make pretty with a little work stand in line.

Sweetie, you are not my friend because you are just OK. You are my friend because you are *stupenda*. You are my friend because you are Alpha Plus.

Girls like you and me, sweetheart, do not – I repeat, do NOT – stand in line.

Here's how it works:

Check out the herd, honey, up towards the head of the line. Look for the most lost loser, the weakest link in the chain. The guy who simply will not BELIEVE that you even know he exists, the guy who will start fingering his rosary the moment you talk to him, just praying you won't disappear. You go right up to him and you put your wet lips right up against his ear, right where your hot breath is going to tickle his tympan, and in the most helpless tone you can come up with, Little Miss Muffet, Little Bopeep, Betty Boop, all rolled into one, you ask please, oh please would he get it for you, like he would even dream of refusing, and then you stand there admiring him as he places the order, like he's just killed a T Rex with his own two hands, and you wait for him to get it, and then, the moment he hands it to you, those beady little eyes of his all hot with hope, while he's still recovering, while he's still under your spell, you say, "Oh that was *so* sweet of you, I will *never* forget this," and then, you RUN, do not hesitate, RUN before he can so much as ask your name.

And voila! Mission accomplished. Line ignored.

See? It's easy. But the one thing you never do – are you listening? do you hear this? – you NEVER stand in line.

Cheryl Makes Her Tape

My name is Cheryl. I'm twenty-four. I'm originally from
Pittsburgh. I went to a two-year college. Mt. Bushie, up in
Massachusetts. I majored in psychology....Uh... What else?... I
work as a receptionist at a small company in Midtown. Very small.
Actually, it's just me and my boss... It's only temporary. At least, it
was supposed to be. I couldn't believe how hard it was to find a job
here. And New York is so expensive. At least, on my salary...Oh
right, that reminds me. I live in a one bedroom. I share it with
another girl. Woman. You're supposed to say woman up here,
aren't you? Anyway, her name is Joanie. She's got the bedroom. I
don't really think that's fair. You'd think we could trade or
something. At least when guys come over. Not that I have any
guys over. I mean, that's why I'm here. Oh God, I shouldn't have
said that. Now whoever listens to this will think I'm desperate. I'm
not, really. At Mt. Bushie, I had more dates than a lot of girls. Of
course, no one had too many. I mean, it was all girls, for Pete's
sake. Forget it. All I mean is, it's hard here. To meet people. That's
why I'm doing this. I said that, didn't I? Even Joanie has trouble,
and she's pretty. Not that I don't think I'm pretty... Wait a minute.
Can we turn this off for a minute?.. Are you sure? ..Well, OK. I
just don't want to look stupid is all.

Where was I? Joanie. Yes. Joanie has hardly any more dates than
me. And she's got a bosom. With a capital 'B'. That's sort of what
it looks like, actually. Like you blew up a 'B' and strapped it on
sideways. Oh God, why am I talking about my roommate's
breasts? Now you're going to think I'm a lesbian. And on top of
that I went to Mt. Bushie. An all girl's school. Like I don't know
what everybody says about those places. But that's ridiculous!
Look, I wouldn't be here if I didn't like men, right?

At least, sometimes I do. They really can be pigs. Like they're doing you a favor by tugging at your underwear. Not that I'm frigid or anything. Don't get me wrong. If people only knew. But when you meet some one at Friday's and you end up in a doorway and things get a little intimate, just because you didn't get what you wanted then and there, well there was a taxi idling across the street, for Pete's sake, and it was late, but there were people coming by, that's not so hard to understand, is it? So after all that why take somebody's number if you're not going to call? That's what I don't get. What's so hard about picking up the phone?...

Well, anyway, my hobbies are needlework and going to the movies, and I'm really looking forward to meeting some new people, especially since this is costing me an arm and a leg.

I guess that's it.

Did I do OK?

Spectator Spurt

That guy's always looking at girls. Look at him. Jesus. He should have a turret instead of a neck. That poor girl. Do you think she even knows he's checking her out? Look at that. It's like he's licking her with his eyes. Ewwww! We'd better find him a towel before he gets drool all over the floor.

And she's not even that pretty. Well, she's not. Look at her. Completely synthetic product, on top of that. You think those are real? Oh come on! Not that round they're not. No way. Though I guess they do make her butt look smaller. So maybe the... uh... enhancement was a good move. I mean, she'd look like a freakin' bowling pin otherwise.

Please. Don't tell me that's all big bones. Too many frappucinos, if you ask me. Two words, honey: work-out.

Or is that one word? Is work-out one word?

Not to mention those lips. Jesus. Any more collagen and they'd explode.

Though they do make her nose look smaller. There's always that. But on the other hand, now her eyes look even tinier. Got yourself a dilemma there, sweetie. Can't really win either way.

Oh my God, look at that. He's actually talking to this one. He really likes her. He really thinks she's hot.

God, men can be so disgusting sometimes. They really can.

Be Yourself

The important thing is to be yourself. That's all. It's that simple.

Take you, for instance. You're sitting here listening to me very intently, nodding wisely now and then, acting very interested... Because we're talking about a Serious Subject. A Heavy Subject. And you're doing a very good job of looking me in the eye.

Except when I look away and you think I can't see you. Then you steal a peek at my breasts. Because what you really want to do is sleep with me. You don't give two figs for what I'm talking about. I could be translating Sanskrit into Farsi for all you care. I could be reciting the Periodic Table backwards in Urdu. And you'd still have exactly the same expression of rapt interest. And you'd still be just praying for me to glance out this window or watch somebody walking in, so you could get another good gander at the twins here.

(Say hello to the nice man, girls.)

I don't even want to think about what would happen if I had to bend over and tie my laces.

And what I'm trying to say here is, that's you. Well, within legal limits. I'm guessing the really real you would have all your clothes off by now and would be down on your hands and knees whimpering, absolutely pleading for me to rut like a monkey. Right here, right now, and damn the cappuccino.

Did you want to do that? Don't let me stop you. Because the important thing is to be exactly who you are.

That's all I'm saying. Just be yourself.

Lily

That lily. It's shivering.

Did you see that?

Why would it do that? I don't feel a breeze. Do you?

It's so pretty. White, fluted. Opening up its throat to the world.

Why would it tremble like that? The ground's not shaking, is it? If it is, I didn't notice. I usually notice those things. I'm very sensitive, you know. Oh yes. I can tell when it's about to rain. Just by the taste of the air. That's right. The taste.

Look, it did it again!

Oh no… You missed it. It's not moving now. Now it's perfectly still.

But you don't notice things like that, do you? They don't bother you. You go right on with what you're doing.

I'm not like that myself. I pick up on things. I notice.

I was always like that. It's true. Since I was little.

The other children thought I was very strange. It was awful. Can you believe that? Oh, yes. They could be terribly cruel. Terribly, terribly cruel.

Oh God, it's doing it again. – I'm telling you I saw it.

I can't believe you didn't notice. You really didn't notice that? Honestly?

I just don't understand you sometimes.

Floppy

I was gonna put your stuff on a floppy disk, by the way. But I forgot to get one.

That's what happens when you're on drugs.

Just kidding.

Anyway, I found it all. As soon as I get a disk, I'll copy it over. Then we're done.

Right?

Of course, I could e-mail them to you. Then we wouldn't even have to see each other, right?

Just kidding.

I'm not myself. I'm a little out there.

But I'm fine. Don't worry. I'm good.

It's not a problem.

You left some pictures by the way. On the hard drive. Is that what you liked? You could have told me. I might…

No. Probably not. I don't think I would have. But maybe if you'd told me…

The rest of it, it was all where you said it would be. I knew it would. If you're one thing, it's organized.

In fact, I'll bet you're a little irritated at me, aren't you? Because I didn't have the disk. And this was supposed to be it. This was supposed to be the end.

Not that you said that. No, no. Just, "Hey, listen, do you think you could you bring me those files?" Those files which were exactly where you said they would be. Of course. And you had it all planned out, and all I had to do was bring the disk.

Look, I didn't do it on purpose. No, no, I know. You didn't say you were mad.

It's just, like I said, I'm not myself lately.

Salsa Picante

Ow, that burns!

That's really hot. How do you eat that stuff?

I'm not that adventurous. Don't get me wrong. I like trying new things. But this isn't something I'd want everyday, you know? It's too intense. That's more than I want to deal with on a regular basis. Most of the time, I just want to eat. Just stuff my face. It's not like I'm trying to learn all the time. Sometimes you just want to be, you know. Just work with what you got.

Is that wrong? Do you disapprove? I know you didn't say so. But it's something about you. You make me feel like I should be trying. For what, I'm not exactly sure. Just trying. Like no one has the right to rest. To be happy where they are.

This is the kind of thing you like. Sharp. Burning. The sudden surprise on your tongue. It's not like you can ignore it. You have to deal with it. Taste it. Swallow it. Grab a glass of water afterwards.

And you like that, don't you? That it makes you work. That it doesn't just let you sit there.

I'm glad you like it. And I guess it's why I like you. But it's not the only way to live, you know.

It's not the only way to live.

Starlite

Starlite! No! Bad puppy!

Starlite, stop that! You're scaring the man! Quiet, honey. Calm down. Calm down, sweetie.

She never does this. I don't know what's gotten into her. – Stop it, honey. Now stop that, right now.

I can't understand. She's normally not like this at all. – Pup! Puppy! Baby! – Don't worry. She makes a lot of noise, but she won't...–

Starlite! Get away from that man's leg! You stop that! Close those jaws right now!

Do you think you could move back just a little? Just a little, OK?

Oh my God, she's getting so upset. Oh honey. What's the matter baby? Did you think the big bad man was going to hurt Mommy? Oh honey, calm down. It's OK.

You must be in her territory. That's what's upsetting her. Well, I mean it's her territory for now. Just for...

Starlite, no!

Look do you want to upset her? Just get back, OK? I told you, she thinks you're in her territory. And that just makes her –

Oh no! Oh Starlite! Oh God, no!

Young lady! Open those jaws right now! Right now, young lady!

Well, I'm sorry. If you hadn't upset her so. Oh, come here darling. Oh honey!

C'mon, it's not that deep. Don't be such a big baby.

That's all right, honey. The bad man upset you, didn't he? Yes, yes, he did. That's OK, sweetie. No, no, no. That's a good puppy.

You didn't do anything wrong.

Always There

I don't have any horror stories about my father. No repressed memories or anything like that. He fed us, he clothed us, he loved us. And made it seem as simple as that.

My uncle, his younger brother, was bitter and restless. Once when my cousin got angry at me, she said, "Your father is boring! He doesn't want to do anything but get along! Daddy says he's a complete failure!" She thought she'd upset me with this. But instead I laughed. Just laughed my heart out. Because my father was exactly who he wanted to be. I couldn't believe she didn't see that.

Her father was hardly there. My uncle left her and her mother and sister when she was small. Supposedly because he had this big opportunity to do a film. It never happened. But even when he came back here, he never did move back with them.

It's true, I suppose, to the outside world. Now that I'm older, I know that. He's never done anything important. At least to anyone else. But my sister's got three kids, my brother's just had his first, and I'm getting married next month. Because we all want families like the one we grew up in. We want to build new rooms on that first solid house, a house where we came home and our father was always there.

YOUNGER ADULT: Male

Hi There

OK if I sit here?

Excuse me, I said, is it OK? Hey, I'm just trying to be polite. Whoa. Sorry to bother you.

But since you don't mind…

Hey, don't worry about me. You just go ahead and do what you were doing.

Don't mind me.

Pretty private type, huh? Oh I understand. I spend a lot of time by myself too. Lots. Understand perfectly.

Sometimes people just want to be left alone.

Nice of you to let me sit here anyway.

No, I mean it. Some people get really touchy when you ask to sit down. Cop a whole attitude and stuff.

Oh yeah.

But you see, you didn't do that. 'Cause you're OK. A little quiet, looks like, but OK.

You know, I kind of like you. No, no, it's not like you have to say anything. I can just tell.

Want to do something sometime?

Oh, I know, it's a little premature. I mean, I don't even know your name.

Want to know mine? It's –

Wait, wait. Where are you going? No, no, you don't have to leave. No, no, wait. That's –

Well. Nice meeting you anyway.

Hey there. Looking for a seat? You're welcome to share my table.

Sure, come on. Sit down. Oh, don't worry about me.

I'm not much of a talker.

The Help

Yes. May I help you?

Uh… before you answer, let me clarify that. When I say "help", that means, "sell you something".. In fact, it means, sell you as much as I can. It most certainly does not indicate any interest in your problems generally, so please, if you've had a bad day, don't share. In fact if anything I'd be prepared for that trend to continue, should you be so unwise as to demand more than the absolute minimum of my otherwise unoccupied time.

Nor might I add, does the phrase "May I help you?" indicate the slightest interest in your more esoteric needs; to whit, which nuance of color, taste or exotic origin will especially satisfy your secret sense that you are special, you are not like the others, you have refinements of sensitivity that require the most exquisite care and effort from such minions as ourselves, who exist after all – at least in the regal corridors of your own mind, which are no doubt lined with the largest of mirrors – who exist, I say, only to cater to your putrid little whims.

Regrettably, we exist, as it happens, to draw a salary, with which miserable pittance we will struggle to attain the exalted heights for which we are secretly destined. Or, failing that, drink ourselves silly in an effort to forget how we spend our days.

Waiting, that is, – can you stand it? – on the likes of you.

Now. Do we have that perfectly clear? To review: We are here to sell you things. You are here to give us money. For all else, please look under "C" for "Care? Don't."

And so, with the ground rules thus clearly defined, allow me to ask you once again, "May I help you?"

The Promo Guy

Oh, did you hear? Fenton died. You know, the goofy guy from the record company? Skinny, always wearing a suit. Can you beat that? Trying to push rock and roll, and you're wearing a suit?

I guess you didn't notice he hadn't been around. Fenton was like that. You'd walk in and he'd be there and you had to remind yourself to notice him. Not to seem rude, you know? But he didn't exactly grab your attention.

Imagine that. A promo guy, and the best thing he knew how to do was be invisible. He should have been in the CIA. They need people like that. – Record companies, on the other hand, don't generally consider it a plus.

Anyway, here's what happened. He heard a noise in the apartment next to his. This was in the afternoon. Because, of course, he was home a lot. He wasn't what you'd call a go-getter. And he knew his neighbor wasn't home. So he went to check it out. And there's these two guys in there, and they're wrapping her stereo in a towel.

So what does he do? Run back inside, lock his door and call the police? Not Fenton. He has to stop them. He steps into the doorway and tells them to put the stuff down.

Can you imagine anything more idiotic? Isn't that just like him?

Especially because, well, he wasn't what you'd call scary looking. Plus, one of these guys, turns out when they caught him, he was huge. So what's he do? He gives Fenton a shove, right on the shoulder. Just to get him out of the way. Only Fenton, that klutz, he goes flying backwards, right down the stairs.

And snap! Breaks his neck. Just like that.

Then these guys took off. But like I said, they caught them later.

Isn't that just like him, though, to do something so idiotic? Bet he thought he'd be a big hero.

What a loser. Right to the end.

Hey, while I've got you here, you gotta hear this tune. The new guy brought it in. Man, I'm telling you, it is going to KILL you!!

Super Squirrel

See that squirrel over there? Busy little fella, ain't he?

Whoa! Now that was a leap. Didn't think he'd make that one.

He's looking at us. Hey squirrel! Hey sweetie! Over here.

Whoa! What was that? Did you see that? He hissed at me.

Now that's scary.

Look at that. He's watching us. Like we were made out of acorns. I do not like that look.

What the hell is up, squirrel? This is no way to make friends with the dominant species, let me tell you.

You think we're in his territory? Do squirrels even have territory?

Oh my God! He hissed again. Did you see those TEETH?

Get back, you! Shoo! Go away!

I can't believe it! He's ignoring me. Like I'm not ten times his size. What? You think I can't hurt you? Huh? Get back! Shoo!

Oh Jesus, it's like he's heard of the ASPCA. Like he knows I wouldn't dare touch him. But he can hurt me, can't he? With those teeth! Are you kidding?

He HISSED again!

He's sick! That's gotta be it! That's why he's so aggressive! Oh my God, he's going to bite me! That's why he keeps coming forward.

Get back, you damn disease vector! Stay the hell away from me!

Listen to that hissing! And all he has to do is leap from there!

Well, I mean, he's sick, right? That'll give him extra strength, won't it? At least until he just keels over from... Mad Squirrel Disease, or whatever it is.

Watch out!!! He's about to – WHOA!

Whoa...

Did you see that? Right up into that tree. How the hell he'd do that?

That is really something. Go, squirrel!

No, but seriously. That squirrel should have an 'S' on his chest. 'Cause I'm here to tell you: that there's onw Super Squirrel.

Straight Up

I just think women should be more honest. Straightforward. You know, like guys.

The thing is, our first date went so well. I'm serious. We got along great. So I asked her out again. To a concert. OK, she didn't like the music. Not that she said so. But I could tell. I'm pretty sensitive. You know, for a guy.

So I asked her out again. She had to work. Fine. Waited a few days, called again. Her brother's in town.

Now at this point, my friend, he's saying, "She's letting you down easy, man. She's just not into you." Well, the hell with that. Because, if that's how it is, she should just say so, right?

I call her again. Same thing. My friend says, "Dude, just leave it alone." But I'm sorry. I'm not like that. You have something to tell me, you tell me straight up. I'm sorry. That's just how I am.

So. I called and I got her machine. Fine. I left her a message, short and sweet. "Look, you keep saying you want to see me, but it's like, you're always busy. So which is it? Do you or don't you? All I'm saying is, be straight with me. Cause that's just a matter of respect."

See? I put it on the table. Laid it straight out. Because that's me. That's how I am.

Next day, I come home and there's a message. It's from her.

"You want me to be clear? OK, here's clear. I am not attracted to you physically. I am not attracted to you mentally. I don't like the way you dress, I don't like the way you talk, I don't like the way you think. In fact, I'm not entirely sure I like YOU. Not only do I have no desire to go out with you, I don't even want to be your friend."

"Is that straight enough? Any questions? Good. Bye."   And she hung up. Hard.

But you know what? I think that's great. I think that is so cool. Because she was straight with me. Right out. Cards on the table. Just like a guy.

Why can't more women be like that?

Home Schooling

It's not your fault. Come on, Mom, stop that now. You're gonna make me feel bad. And let me tell you, doing twenty-five years, I feel pretty bad already.

Look, you did your best. And you did it all by yourself. You think I'm ungrateful. But I'm not. I know how hard you worked. Jesus, two jobs at once, more often than not. How could you know what I was up to? You couldn't. Even when you got home, you were so damn tired. You didn't even have time to talk, did you? You could barely get down a bite before going to bed.

I understand that. It was hard. How could you be at work and at home at the same time? You couldn't. I know that.

But look. What I did, where I've ended up? You can't blame yourself. It's not like I learned it from you. My friends were the ones who got me here. They taught me about how to have the wrong kind of fun, how to get in trouble, how to not care about how it came out. I learned it all from them. I wanted to make them happy, to impress them. I was their prize pupil. 'Cause they cared about me, you know? Cause they're the ones who gave me applause. They're the ones who smiled when I did it right. When I did wrong right.

It's not like you taught me any of this. How could you? What could I ever have learned from you?

You were never there.

ADULT: Female

Can Opener

He took the damned can opener.

It's a trial separation, for Gods sakes. All he had to do was take some clothes and his toothbrush. And a few pieces of furniture, like his desk and that one chair. God, how he loves that chair. But it's not like he's moving out entirely, dammit. He's still got all his books here, and his stereo, and most of his clothes too, as far as that goes.

Why would he take the can opener?

Oh, it's not a big deal. Why the hell even think about a can opener anyway? Until you need some tuna fish, that is. Then... Then, let me tell you, you think about it. There it is, all that tightly packed, oily flesh, firm and tasty, right there, ready to fill you up. Except... Except you're not getting any. Because you know what? You don't have a damned CAN OPENER!!!

That's right, fully equipped kitchen, microwave, Viking range, Sub-zero fridge, Miele dishwasher, full set of All-Clad pots and pans, full set of Mikasa dishes... and none of it's worth a damn thing because right now you really, really want just one thing, one little thing that you really, really like. Sure it's not fancy, in fact it's pretty simple, damned straightforward really, but it just happens to be exactly what you crave, right now, only now, now you can't have it, because there's NO CAN OPENER!!!

Men! Did I mention they can be really inconsiderate?

Sensei Susan

Right off, you've got an advantage. You're a woman. They'll think you're weak. Good! Use that! They'll come right at you. Don't be afraid; be a windmill. The wind hits those fragile blades with all its strength and what do they do? They take that power for their own. By moving. By adapting. And yet: the windmill stands, one with the ground.

Don't mistake acceptance for surrender. Take what comes at you, but on your own terms. Transform it. Turn it into what you need. Re-direct a punch, sidestep a lunge. Send that strength the way YOU want it. Spin the wind towards the ground. But don't flee and don't flinch. Know who you are and what you can do.

Remember! You're a woman. They'll think you're weak....

The Insult

That guy didn't look at me.

No, no, you don't understand. They always look. Doesn't matter if I'm in a baggy sweatshirt with curlers in my hair. They look.

Until I glare at them. Or tell them where to go. And even then sometimes, they'll just laugh like it's a big joke. And then go right on staring, getting themselves an eyeful.

Oh, it's not like I let 'em get away with it. Don't think that. But the point is, I'm the one who tells them to quit it. I'm the one who calls time out.

Not them. Never them.

On top of that, he was right at eye level. It's not like he had to crane his neck. He had a ringside seat.

And he didn't even look. He didn't even twitch.

Do you think he's…. Oh hell, even they look. Come on, this is worth it. This is serious business here. This is the real goods.

Not a glance. Not a flutter.

That is so not right. That is just wrong.

I'm going to say something. No, I am. I'm sorry, but that's just plain rude.

Maybe if I walked by him? Slowly?

The Author

Why Albert, how lovely to hear from you!

No, no, don't be silly. That was years ago. No hard feelings at all.

Why yes, I am. Very well indeed. Hard at work on my third novel. As I'm sure you heard, the first two did rather well.

Well, thank you. That's very kind. Especially since I'm sure it came as a big surprise.

Oh, don't you? As I recall, "Wasting your time on that crap" was the phrase you used. But I'm sure you meant well by it.

Now where did you hear that? I do not use my old boyfriends in my work. It's all out of my own little head. Pure fiction.

Well, yes, That's what Howard claimed, but it was nonsense. Anyway, he lost the case. Very hard to sue an author, you know. It really is.

So tell me, Albert, did you ever work out that little potty problem of yours?

Goodness, no need to get so upset. Dear boy, it's hardly your fault if your mother never taught you proper hygiene. WIth the life she led, how was she to find the time?

Not at all! I admired your mother. Not that she thought much of me, did she? But she lived her life to the fullest and right she was. Why should a woman ignore her own needs just because she has a husband and a son? – How is your father by the way? Did he get that pardon?

At any rate, you've got quite the reputation now too, haven't you? I'm so glad to hear that. That you're smack in the middle of the public eye. You can't imagine how it delights me to hear that.

Not at all, Albert. As I said, that's all in the past. I was young, inexperienced. And far too vulnerable. It was a learning experience. It's made me the woman I am today. To tell you the truth, I had rather forgotten you. But now that we've talked, it's all coming back. All of it.

Well, I should get back to work. I must say, I was a little stuck this morning. But I think I've got a few ideas now. Let me jot them down while they're still fresh.

No, no, honestly. I can't tell you how glad I am you called.

Just Dessert?

What's the point of being single if you can't have fun? That's what I always say.

So it's not like I'm looking to stop. Why would I do that? I like that part. I like it as much as they do.

Only, how come that's all there is? It's like they step into the trap for an instant, and then, zoom, they're out the door. Like they're scared. Can you believe it? Scared of me?

I'm not scary, am I? I'm friendly. I'm a good time. Why would they be scared of *me*?

It wasn't always like that, let me tell you. I dated guys who had boats. And bought me necklaces. Just like that. Right after lunch, "Why don't we go next door? I'll buy you some pearls." Bam! A thousand bucks. No questions asked. It wasn't like he was trying to get something. *He already got it!* This was after. And he came back for more. Plus, he was gorgeous.. Long blond pony tail, hot bod. And he liked me. He hung around.

It's not like this was a long time ago, either. Two, three years. What, I suddenly got ugly and nobody told me?

Now, I end up with all these losers. Don't get me wrong. They're not bad guys. Just because they're broke. They've got other things going for them. But still, you'd think they'd be a little grateful, no? Enough to stick around for seconds.

Instead... Well, what is it, can you tell me? Why are they so scared of me?

Order

What can I get for you, hon'? Sandwich? Salad? We got some ribs.

Take your time. No hurry.

Some pasta maybe? With lemon and basil?

Tired, huh? Rough night? Oh, I know how that is.

Turkey, maybe? Fresh baked. All white and moist. Be nice on rye. Little lettuce. Little mayonnaise. Or wheat maybe. Sourdough? Whole grain? French? Take your pick. We got 'em all.

No, no. No hurry. No hurry at all.

So, what was it last night? Party? Movie premiere? One of those things where they open up the galleries? You really get out, don't you?

Me, not so much. I got my kids, the job. You know how it is. Got to pay the bills.

Like tuna? We did it special today. A little curry and raisin. It's nice. It is. I tasted it earlier.

Hey, don't fall asleep on me now! We gotta get some lunch in you.

What about the grilled veggies? Little olive oil on the side. Simple, good for you.

Not to be personal, but... I see you here a lot. And at that coffee bar over there too.

That must be nice. Not to have to work. For a while anyway. I think I'd get bored myself. With nothing I'd exactly have to do. Then I figure the small things start to become a big deal. Because, well, that's all you have to do all day, is decide what to have for lunch. For instance.

Might as well enjoy it, huh, if it's all you've got to do. Might as well take your time.

Some paté maybe? With a few of those little French pickles? And a nice baguette?

That's OK. Don't rush. I understand.

These things are important.

The Hawk

I saw a hawk today, hovering over the Pacific. It didn't move for the longest time, just hung there, its wide wings still, still as the vast blue water below. As still as if it hung from a string.

How do they do that, birds? Stay perfectly still in the air, with no effort?

It gave me something to think about, instead of you. I didn't want to think about you. Then I would have wondered when you'd come, or if you'd come, or – well, you know, the whole parade. The whole tawdry parade.

And that ocean. You can see why they called it the Pacific. It is peaceful. So much sun on so much blue. It's hard to have complicated thoughts when you look at something so supremely simple.

Don't you think? Don't you agree?

What do you think about, anyway? You never really say. Not really. Oh, you talk well enough. You're a lovely talker. I could listen to you talk all day. But… Well, it's playback, isn't it? From that camera of yours, taking everything in. I never really know who's behind it, framing the shot.

That's quite a trick you have, of seeming to say so much, of seeming to get so carried away. And yet, you haven't moved the whole time, have you? You haven't lifted a feather.

How do you do that, darling? How do you soar so high, yet stay so still?

Trees

Before we sign, I wanted you to know:

I planted all this with my own hands: each tree, each bush, each hedge. When we moved here, this was just one more Connecticut lawn. A handsome lawn: wide, lush, sloping down to a glorious view. Even now, you can see it, through those boughs. But it was a lawn. One more lawn.

I wanted greenery. Tall, erect, varied. Taut masses of thin branches, prickly conifers with mottled trunks, sultry boughs sweeping the air. Everything trim and ordered, with a subtle symmetry. But contained, not confined. An edge of chaos is important: that sprig of white flowers, escaping the hedge; the patch of purple in the crotch of that tree.

I don't look that strong, do I? I'm surprised myself, how much I've been able to handle. All the holes I've dug, the burlap-wrapped roots I've hefted, the branches I've tied back and cut. Over the years, my husband and I had workers in for all the rest – the gazebo, the trellises, that little shed. But the garden I did myself. Every clump of dirt, every shrub, every tree. Right up until last year, I was still at it, doing my best to make this work.

You'd think it had been here forever, wouldn't you? That's how it seems now. Like the land grew it, not me. That's how it is when you work at a thing. It becomes real to you. You forget your own efforts made it. You forget it could end.

The Exclusive

Excuse me. Excuse me? If you'd just give me a minute…
Thanks. This won't take long.

Let me say first how terribly sorry I am about your father. Just
awful. Awful how it happened. I do hope they catch those people.

Now, what I want to know from you is: how do you feel about
that? About your father's murder. Oh my. You look so shocked.
Was that a horrible question to ask? Was it terribly insensitive?

Isn't it astounding how people can ask such questions? How can
they do such things? But then you should understand. You, of all
people.

Oh, excuse me. I'm sorry. You don't remember me, do you?
You interview so many people, don't you? And events change so
quickly. Priorities. That's what counts. What's news today is trash
tomorrow.

But you see, we have talked before. On the phone. Maybe if I'd
agreed to go on camera. As you kept pushing me to. Maybe then
my face would be familiar.

The Collins boy, remember? The toddler who was kidnapped by
those twelve-year-olds? And – well, you remember what they did
to him, don't you? You're not going to make me go into details, are
you?

Though you certainly tried hard enough at the time. All those
caring concerned calls; all those expressions of sympathy. Oh, and
those lovely flowers. With the station's logo on the card. I never
did thank you for those. And all the while, underneath that chipper,
considerate voice of yours, the insistence, the insistence that I give
you an interview. That I give you an exclusive.

Because I wasn't a person to you, was I? I was a story. Just the
latest, hottest story. Until, mercifully, there was that bombing.

Isn't that awful? To be grateful for a bombing? But it did distract
you. It did make you go away.

Now, let me ask, and please don't beg me to leave you alone, please don't ask me to respect your privacy. Just be a good girl and answer the question, the question you kept trying to ask me: how does it feel?

How does it feel when this happens to you?

Charles

Charles says I shouldn't worry about it. Charles says when his boyfriend refuses to talk to him, he knits. Anthony can't stand the clicking and he always ends up saying something. Which leads to a fight. But at least they're talking. And in the end they make up.

Tonight I'm going to burn that jasmine incense that Barry hates and then wait for him to ask me to put it out. Which I won't. And that should get interesting. Because usually I do whatever he wants me to. I'm forever giving in.

Which is something else Charles says I shouldn't do. Because he says I should have self-respect. Because there's no use loving someone else if you don't love yourself. That's what Charles says.

Sometimes I think I should go out with Charles.

Because I always feel better after I talk to him. Better about myself. And stronger too. Like I can handle anything. Even Barry.

How come Love never makes me feel like that? How come I only get that feeling from Charles?

Hero

You're always trying to save people. I used to love that about you when we were kids. The hero. The helper. Who wouldn't want a brother like that?

Except that right now it's starting to seriously irritate me. What's so great about your life, huh? One divorce. About two hundred jobs.

Sure I'm a mess. But I know I'm a mess. I revel in it. I bask in it. It's my continental breakfast. It's my gourmet lunch.

You, Mr. Superior, you're like a house built on stilts. With nothing but mud to hold it up. One good flood, honey, and you're gone.

So don't lecture me on getting my act together, or lying here in the pit. I like my pit. It's never let me down.

But that high-grade education of yours, and all the titles on your business card, they're setting you up for one hell of a fall. You've got a word for each of us, a nice solid piece of advice. But all that does is let you turn your head, turn it away from your own decay.

And the termites are working, honey, they're working hard.

So thanks for the lecture and thanks for sure for the love. There never was that much to go around. But you're the one I'm worried about. You're the one with the distance to fall.

Knocking

One, when I was ten and she was twelve, I had a headache. I went to see the school nurse, but her door was closed. She always did that. We used to call her "Nurse Not-In". Finally, I gave up and went to Allie's class. I was crying by then. She asked the teacher – didn't ask, exactly, but the words were right – if she could be excused, then she got up and came outside.

As soon as I said what was the matter, she took me by the hand and charged down to see the nurse. The door was still closed, but she just kept hammering at it until Nurse Not-In stepped out. "Why Allie," she said, "I'm surprised at you." But Allie just drew herself up until she looked a head taller than she was and said, "Don't you give me that! You're always hiding in there! People have to practically die before you'll open the damned door!" My head was hurting, but still it made me laugh, the way Nurse Not-In stepped back. After that, she gave me my aspirin and she was nice as pie.

That's what Allie was like then. You wouldn't know it now. She's still a spitfire sometimes, but mostly she's just given up. Daddy's death was part of it. And all those lousy men. She just kept choosing the wrong ones to take care of.

Suddenly, I don't know when, I became the strong one. I'm the one with the good job, the nice place. The one thing that's the same is, she won't ask for help. She's the one with the headaches now, and the one closing the door, too. Don't even think about saying she drinks too much. When I'm home, she always gives me a hug and screams how happy she is to see me, and then she just wants to be left alone.

The funny thing is, she still intimidates me, even now. But one day when I've gotten stronger, when I've really become as brave as I look, I'm going to start knocking, good and loud, and I'm not stopping. I'm not stopping until she comes out.

ADULT: Male

Hotel Clerk

Now if you'll just sign the guestbook, we should have the room ready for you soon.

You're so lucky we had this last minute vacancy. As I'm sure you know, the whole town's full up. Pretty much have to take what you can get, isn't that right?

Excuse me one moment. – Officer, are you and your colleagues about done? Good, good. Thank you.

Sorry about that. The local police are excellent. It's very safe here. Oh yes. Very safe.

Let me just buzz Housekeeping and see if they can start cleaning it for you. – Yes, could you check number thirteen and see if those gentlemen from the EMS have left with the bo- the last guest? Thank you.

Oh! Before I forget. You don't mind the smell of bleach, do you? Might be a bit more of it up there then usual, I'm afraid.

Not ideal, I know. But as I say, it is full up in town. Can't be too particular, now can we?

At any rate, with a little luck we'll have you in there in time to freshen up, relax, maybe watch the Six O-Clock – What am I saying? You don't want to watch the news.

Not tonight.

But we do have a nice library of classic films. Do you like Hitchcock? I believe we have one of his. Let me think now…

Oh yes. That one about the shower.

Perhaps you'd prefer the talking rabbits.

Did you see these postcards here? Most of the rooms look just like that. Same beds, same curtains, same carpeting.

Though we'll be putting a rug in yours. A very large rug.

Anyway, as I say, you're very lucky. Very lucky indeed.

We really weren't expecting this vacancy.

Seat-Sighting

I'm sorry, could you move? Yeah, just a little that way. Thanks. I'm trying to look at that girl's butt. This side of it anyway. Muscular, huh? I love it when you get that flat slab of muscle before the curve.

Chest is OK. Oh, you can't see it from here. She was walking towards me before. It's that black sweater that does it. Kind of frames the picture, if you know what I mean.

Damn, she moved again. Do you think you could…? Thanks. Yeah, that's much better.

Oh my God, she's bending over. Jesus. Wait, wait, just a minute. … Oh, my God. Oh dear Lord. I wish you could have seen that. No, DON'T TURN AROUND!! She'll think we're looking at her!

Don't want to spook her, you know?

But let me tell you, that was beautiful. Oh man, that was Rembrandt. Pablo Picasso. Norman Rockwell. Whatever. I'm just saying: it was good.

Aw. She's leaving. No, no, not yet. Just a minute more. Please…

You think she can hear me? Like psychically, I mean? Probably not. Oh well.

I can dream, can't I? Can't I just? Dream.

Snakes

So yeah, it's great to meet you. Stanley may have told you, I don't socialize much. Oh it's not like I don't have fun. I do lots of things. I like to take pictures. Pictures of bones. You know how like when a cat gets hit by a car and it lies by the road for a long time and finally all its fur falls off because the ants eat away all its flesh, and after a while there's nothing left but bones? Those kind of bones. I like to take pictures of those bones.

And I develop them myself. I like the darkroom. All those chemicals, the way they smell. And that red light. Like in the zoo, you know, the room where they keep all the animals that don't like light?

I guess not everybody goes to the zoo that much.

That's another thing I really like. The zoo. Mostly that room with the red lights. They have snakes there. I like snakes. A lot of people don't like snakes. They think they're creepy. But I don't. I think snakes are smart. They're smart because they curl up, all into themselves, like they don't care about anybody else, and then they don't move, not for the longest time. Not until they see something they like.

Well, "like" means they want to kill it.

Maybe "like" isn't exactly the right word.

But anyway, when they see something like that, after being real still for so long, looking like they can't even move, KCHA!, they strike. And they swallow it. Whole. So it's still alive, you know, only now it's inside them. Inside the snake's belly.

And then they just sit there for a really long time, and the whole time their muscles are crushing this thing up and digesting it, this thing that just a minute ago was hopping around and making squeaky sounds.

So, anyway, are you hungry? Want to look at a menu? You ready to eat?

Daddy's Boy

Oh yeah, we love our new son. Do you have a light?

Look at him. Barely human they are at that age. All scrunched up and red. At least his eyes are open now. What are you looking at, you little devil, huh? Is Daddy's smoke bothering you? Oh now, you'll get used to it. Those little fists are just like bunches of worms, aren't they? Grab, grab, grab. Greedy little bugger. Listen to that! Listen to that cough! Oh, 'ou poo-ah 'iddle bubbims. Is 'ou catch cold? He should be OK. That blanket's nice and warm. Cashmere. We got it at Saks. Lovely shade of yellow, isn't it? Like the walls at Monet's place in France. My wife and I were over there last year. Back when we could still travel.

Damn. Now I've done it. That ash'll wash out. It's a shame, though. The blanket's brand new. Oh, honey, did I get some in your eye? Ssh, ssh now. Daddy didn't mean it.

Some babies remind me of fish. Like they were yanked out of the water and slapped onto the land. Little mouths working and sucking in air. This one's the worst. You'd think he had asthma or something. Wheeze, wheeze. What do you think that you are, an accordion? Huh? Huh?

I love these French cigarettes. Pick them up by the carton when I can find'em. They've got body, you know? You can really see the smoke. That nice, dark aroma. Like burning a pile of wet leaves.

Oh, what a face! My son, the troll. You'd think he'd been soaked in formaldehyde. Come on, now. Smile for Daddy. Smile and take a deep breath.

Trust

You can't trust a soul. Simple truth.

See that space? Used to be a radio there. Nice. AM-FM, cassette, CD. The works. Had it for two months.Stole it from a friend. Long story. He owed me. Trust me. Would I lie to you?

Anyway, I watched out for him. You betcha. Wouldn't let him near my truck. What do I look, stupid?

Trouble is, I was watching too hard. One day, I see him lurking around. Skulking, like, you know? So I go, "Oh no you don't, I'm keeping my eye on you."

I see him duck around my neighbor's place. My neighbor, he's a piece of work. Remind me to tell you about him sometime.

That's his lawnmower right there. Under that tarp.

Anyway, my friend – Oh yeah, we're friends. For real. We hang out. – My friend's gone around there and I figure I better keep an eye cocked. So I follow, and I watch him. I watch him for a long time. But I can't figure out what he's doing.

Screwing me. That's what he's doing. Giving it to me crooked in a tight place. The whole time, I'm watching him – like he knew I would, can you beat that? He sure had me pegged – another one of our friends, Charlie – Same guy got me my TV, only I was supposed to like tip him, you know? And I didn't, because, well, c'mon, you think he paid the place where he boosted it? – Charlie's in my truck, yanking wires, slick and fast.

Cause he's a pro, is Charlie. You want something ripped, that you can trust him to do. And next time I'll know. I come back and, son of a bitch, it's gone. My nice fancy radio, hours of listening pleasure, gone just like that. – Can you beat that? Of all the low-life tricks.

Anyway, that's enough of that. Why don't you come over tonight? We're having a barbecue. Everybody's gonna be there. All my friends, Charlie, everybody. – Bring that new sports car. The white one. Oh, you can park it on the street. Sure. It'll be fine.

Trust me.

Pug Hoskins' Lullaby

Yeah, every mother wants to kill her kids. You kiddin' me? What do you think, little brat half splits her apart gettin' born, wakes her at the wolf hour with a piercing scream, gets his cacadoodle all over her nice clean hands, every night runnin' first year he's here? What do you think that leads to? All tenderness and kindness? "Come here honey, give Mommy a kiss"? It's a wonder more of the bleary-eyed, sleep-deprived guardians of the cubs of our kind don't pick the little honkers up in mid-oratorio and brain them against the bassinet. What would you do to a TV that suddenly switched itself on at 2 A.M. and started blaring battle cries? How long would that wonder of technology last, huh?

OK, so most Moms exhibit a little self-control. Sure they'll fall for a smile or a bit of out-of-the-blue brilliance. You think the rest of that stuff just goes away? You think their nerves suddenly go slack? You think they kick back and listen to harps on high? You think they ever forget that the little darling could explode at any moment into sounds or frowns or bodily fluids, or simply break the Waterford to hear it crash? You think they relax their vigilance, allow their blood pressure a lull? No way. Somewhere inside them, the army's ready. Somewhere battalions of brain cells are on alert. And let the wrong siren go off at the wrong milli-second, those troops might crack a baton on the first little rioter they see.

Of course, most of the time it's more subtle. Sing the kid some nursery rhyme about falling out of a tree. Let him watch cartoons where fluffy little birds sidestep huge claws. Tickle his tender little belly, which is to say poke him hard in his most vulnerable spot, and watch him laugh his defenseless little heart out. Anyway you cut it, the point gets made.

So not every mother pops their kid in the garbage chute. Or whispers good night with a forty-five. Not every grape makes it to the wine either. But all it takes in either case is a little extra squeeze, and the right kind of fermenting in the right kind of darkness.

The Gourmet

No, no, I'll just keep my coat on. It's an... affectation of mine. But I am ready to order, thank you.

What I would like is your osso buco Milanese accompanied by a bottle of the Mastroberadino with – oh why not? – just a dish of escargot to start. Oh, don't worry about money. No problem. Really. I never concern myself with it.

I'm sorry. Is there something the matter with your nostrils? Anyway, money. Not a concern! Why look at me. I don't even shop. Perfectly happy with the clothes I have. Though I suppose that's why that rather nouveau couple over there is examining me so. Really wish they wouldn't. Damn rude. The wife, especially. Do you think you might – ever so tactfully of course – request that she not make such disagreeable faces? You'd think I had an odor or something. Quite impossible, let me assure you. I applied a good swath of roll-on just before I came. Couldn't quite manage a shower, I'm afraid. Lodging difficulties, you know. Not much running water just now. Never worry about these things myself. Just not a materialist, is all.

Oh my, truffles! I just noticed those. Oh I'll take a plate of those, oh yes I will! In fact, make it two, why don't you? Money's no object. Really. Don't give it a second thought.

I never do.

Stress

It's the stress.

Edward insisted on helping me. That's understandable. I'm his dad. He wants to do things with me. That's only natural.

Though, in a way, he's more his mom's kid. That's a horrible way to put it. But it's true. It's not like I planned to be a father. Her? Who the hell knows what she was thinking. Don't ask me. Next thing I know, bang, she's pregnant. "We should get married," she says. "No," I said, "I don't think we should."

Do I look stupid? Tell me, do I look that stupid?

So I say she should get an abortion. Not that I insisted or anything. But there's two of us involved here. We should both have a say. "No way," she said. "I'm having this kid. With you or without you." Not because she didn't believe in it. Nothing like that. Just because. To mess me up.

And then for years, all I saw was bills. Almost. Oh she'd bring him over sometimes. Just enough to make sure he knew he had a father. So she could tell him what a bastard I was.

Until he got old enough to think for himself. Then he started asking questions. And he started wanting to see me.

Suddenly, out of the blue,, she said, "He should live with you." "What?" I said. "It's only fair," she said. "I need a life too. And he's yours as much as mine."

What could I do? He moved in. Suddenly, she, the big loving mommy, she's almost never around. Because she wants to have fun, she does. And maybe find another sucker.

He's an OK kid. A little nervous, a little watchful. Talks too much. But he's OK.

It's just, it's a lot of pressure. And this morning I wasn't in the mood. A lot of stuff: bills, work. Trying to be a father. Trying to be a good father.

What happened was, I was working on my new CD burner. Trying to get it working. That's a touchy process, you know? Complicated. And, as it happens, he knows computers. Kids today. They're good at that stuff. And he saw that I was doing it wrong. I was about to put the power cable in backwards. Which I was. He was right. And he said, "Watch it, Dad that's…" And right away, don't ask me why, right away, I blew up at him. "Don't try to help Edward! I don't want you here, OK? Just get out of my life, OK? Just leave me ALONE."

I felt bad the moment I said it. I did. But I figured it would be better if I talked to him later.

Bad move, I guess.

We should find him. I don't know where he could have gone. His mom's in Hawaii. But we should really find him.

You don't think he'll hurt himself, do you?

Lifesaver

Tommy D. called me this afternoon.

Remember before we got married and I was telling you about all the guys in my old neighborhood. How most of them didn't make it? The guys who overdosed, the guys who went to jail, the guys who got shot. And how I started right down the same road. How I almost ended up like them.

And you asked me how come I didn't? How come I turned out like I did? Even before I found the Lord. Someone took me off the path that I was on, and kept me alive to find the path to Grace. And I told you that someone was Tommy D.

That's what I said back then: that most likely I'd be dead, if it hadn't been for Tommy D.

We hadn't talked for what, ten years? Not that I ever forgot him. But with the business, church… It's been a new life. It's like I put the old one in a jar, screwed the cap on tight and shoved it way back on a shelf.

But Tommy knew how to find me. He always was good that way. He acted all loose and easy going, but he always knew what he wanted. He didn't miss a trick. Not Tommy D.

So he called me at the office, and asked how things were going. He'd heard I got religion and married, both. Said he was glad for me, that those were good things. That he was happy to see how I'd turned out.

Then he said he needed a favor. And right away I knew what it would be.

"Some kids are accusing me," he said. "They went to the police." And I didn't say anything.

"Look," he said, "I need you to be a character witness. I need you to tell them I'm not like that. You know, with the young guys."

Already, I was wishing he hadn't called. And I thought of praying for guidance. But I knew I didn't have to. Not this time.

"I can't do that, Tommy," I said.

"Why? Why the hell can't you?" I'm sure he didn't mean to shout. But he was panicking. You could hear that. That he really needed me to do this.

"Because you are like that," I said. "And you know it. You do do those things. Just like they're saying. You do."

And he didn't even argue, you know? He couldn't. He couldn't tell me it wasn't true. Not me.

And that was that.

I don't regret it. I know I did the right thing.

But you gotta understand. 'Cause I really mean this, with all my heart.

This is the guy who saved my life.

The Choice

Now, you don't have to do this. I want to make that clear.
We're leaving it entirely up to you.

Oh, we'd be disappointed, I won't lie to you. We're doing our
part and we hope you'll do yours. That's only fair. And I'm sure
you'll agree.

We have a lot of power. We know more people than you
probably even knew were out there. We know who they are, where
they are and how to get to them. No pressure, ever. But we get
cooperation.

That's what it comes down to. Cooperation.

The best way to put it is, we're good negotiators. We know how
to approach a problem, but without making it a problem. As it
were.

And what we're doing here is, all of this, all this weight we've
got behind us, this entrée, everything really that makes us who we
are – we're bringing this to you, we're handing you the keys, and
we're saying, "Take it. It's your drive. Steer it your way." And
we're doing this with no strings attached. Not a one.

Now, we've made it clear how we'd like this to play. No point in
hiding that. We want to be up front with you. We definitely have a
button we'd like to see you push.

But you're your own person here. You'll check the system,
weigh the odds; get your mind around the pros and cons. And
then? Well, it's your call. Completely your call.

We think you'll make the right decision.

Car Wash

Take the Vette, would you? The black one.

You want to be careful with it. That one's a pain. Oh yeah, I'm telling you. He'll check it. He'll check it top to bottom, left to right. Knows every scratch, every dent. One new mark and he'll be on you like a fly on a stinkie. Trust me. And dry it good, OK? He'll check for drops. He will. On the hood, on the trunk. On the bumper. Hell, I'm surprised he doesn't pop the hood and check the motor.

Who knows why? It's how some people are. Pain in the brain! Want to let you know they've got the eye. That they're keeping track. Makes them feel like they're a cut above, I guess. Puts them on their little throne.

Still, he's got the Vette and we're got the ones washing it right? There's always that. Something to think about. Maybe it's important. Maybe that's the price of admission. Never quite being happy. Always on the look out for that little ding.

Is it worth the money, you think? Is it worth the car? To live like that. Always on the look-out. Always checking up. Expecting perfection in a messed up world.

Don't know. Wouldn't work for me.

Would it work for you? What do you think? Is that any way to live?

Psyche

You know it's not my fault, right? Because this time I was ready to commit. 100 %. Honest. My bachelor days were as good as done.

The plan was, while I was down here, she'd be looking for a house. It had to be big enough for Psyche. Psyche's a sweet dog, but she's touchy about change. It's just a bit much for her in certain respects.

So I'm down here, and I'm packing my apartment, and she calls me. Turns out she's found the perfect place. Only, it won't be free for another six months. But that's OK, she tells me, because we can stay in the studio in the meantime. And I ask, "What about Psyche?"

Then she tells me, well, I can find someone to take care of her for six months. Six months! I know Psyche's not going to like that.

So, OK, I try to explain that, and I'm getting nowhere. Then suddenly I realize: she wants me to get rid of Psyche. That's what's really going on. She doesn't want to live with the dog.

Now, I didn't get a dog to be disposable. I don't understand how anyone can have a pet and not have a strong emotional attachment to it.

So far everything's been fine until the dog. We had a fun summer. And since then too. She's been perfectly fine except about this one little thing. But this is an issue I'm not willing to compromise on.

I've pretty much told her, she hasn't left me much choice. And she, she can't believe I'm not putting the relationship above the dog. But basically, if she's not willing to work this one thing out, I don't think I can get back together with her.

It may work out. But right now, let me tell you, it looks like it's back to me and Psyche.

Confession

I found the Lord! – *Praise the Lord*! – He turned me from my sins! – *Praise Him!* – Killing, robbing. Worse... – *Praise His Name!* – And I was healed – *Yes!* – And when my parole board saw, they saw that I was changed! – *Praise Jesus!* – They saw the Light of His Grace shining on me – *Shining BRIGHT, Lord!* – And they released me. Praise God in His Heaven, they put me back out on the street.

And in the street, I did NOT return to my former ways. I walked in His path and I spoke of His Word and I worked where He willed I work – hauling garbage, cleansing the sick, preparing the dead. I carried the Cross He put on my shoulder and I bent beneath the weight of its Joy.

And when I saw a child – *a little child!* – I tried to embrace Him, to hold Him to me – *to hold His Holiness!* – I tried to bind His Innocence to me. I cried for His Grace, but He would not come. He ran from my heart's cry, from the sanctified craving of my blood, and so I held Him – *Yes!* – and I squeezed Him – *Yes!* – and I would not release Him – *No!* – in my hunger and my aching, I held Him and I hushed Him, and I prayed that He would hear me; still as He lay, limp between my arms, I prayed until they came.

The Edge Of The Mountain

I didn't come all this way to see you. Don't misunderstand. But I'm glad we ran into each other. I won't lie. I had heard you were living around here. I just thought the town was bigger. Funny, huh?

Anyway, I heard you had some kids. How are they doing? Look like you? Geez, it's good to see you, it really is. I still think about you a lot. Oh not all the time, nothing like that. Hell, it's been ten years. But you do come up. You do. You cross my mind.

It's silly that it didn't work out. It really is. We were good together. We were. Can't understand how something that good fell apart. Can you? Can you understand it? You'll have to explain it to me someday. I've never worked it out. And like I said, I think about it. I think about it a lot.

Maybe it was the house. That place you're living in now – Oh I happened to see it, someone mentioned you lived on the edge of the mountain. Fancy, huh? Pretty pricey, looks like. No way I could have afforded something like that. Not me. I didn't come from money. I didn't have that kind of head start. I could never have bought you a home like that. Hidden away. Tucked away. Like you're hiding. Like you're afraid.

Why would you be afraid? I don't understand. Everybody likes you. I heard that for years after you left. "She was so nice. How'd you let her get away?" It's like they're blaming me. But it's not my fault. Is it? I didn't let you get away. You got. Boy, did you get. Ten years too far for me to find you.

Time enough to get tucked away. Have some kids. Nice kids. They're really nice kids. Really, really nice kids. Not that I'd know. It's not like I've seen them. Up close. I mean, even my running into you. Pure coincidence. Just one of those things that happen, you know?

It's awful the things that happen. It really is. You know?

Need

They're scared of us. Let me tell you. That's a fact. We walk in and you can feel it. They sit a little straighter. Watch our every move. Oh, we matter. You can bet on that. We count.

We walk around, checking the lids, the cans, the freezer. Whatever. I don't care if you go into an emergency room, you're going to find something. It can be disgusting sometimes. You want to throw your shoes away, after. You have no idea.

It's just, it's a lot of travel. Thirty percent, minimum. And you don't get much warning. Two weeks, if you're lucky. It changes all the time, too. That's the worst part. You never really feel like you're home.

Plus, you don't make any friends. Because you're always there to find something wrong. It's not like anyone wants to hoist a few when you get off.

So, that's it. I'll be down here again in a month or two. Before that, I'll be up in Napa. Why don't you drive up? Maybe a weekend?

Something to think about. That's all.

What about yourself? That job fall through? Hey, you'll find something. You're lucky. I envy you. I do. You're young. You've got plans. And pretty, of course. There's that.

But come on. I know things are tight. I know how that is. Look, let me help you. Just a loan. Seriously. Don't worry about it. We all need each other, right? People, I mean. Without other people, what are you, right?

Really. Tell me how much you need.

MATURE: Female

Sidewalk Lil

Where ya goin' in such a hurry?

It's a beautiful day, kiddo. Slow down and smell the friggin' roses.

Look at me. Got arthritis, varicose veins. The gas. It's all I can do to haul my fanny out here and sit myself down. But do you see me complaining? Not on your life. Glad to be kickin' and I'll let the world know it.

How old do you think I am? How old? Ah, forget it. You wouldn't believe me if I told you. Old enough, that's all I'll say. Old enough to know better.

You think I don't know the world's a mess? You think I don't know the whole thing's falling apart? Kiddo, I can see the cracks between the clouds. I wake up waiting for the sky to fall. And then when it doesn't, well, I just haul myself out here and sit myself down. Then I watch for people walking by.

And when they do, I say "hello". And there's some that keep on walkin' and some that say it back. Either way, I win. Because I've made my noise. I've gone out on that limb and I've chirped my song.

That's all you can do, right? Is let the world know you're there. Then go home, go to bed, and hope you both make it back in the morning.

I'm telling you, kiddo, you get to be my age, that's about all you can do.

Bernice

I won the TV!

Everybody in the whole bank wanted that TV. All you had to do was fill out the form. Fill out the form and drop it in. It's not like when they want you to give blood. I can't do that. Scared of needles. All my life. So much as touch me with one and I'm out. Just like that.

Anyway, look at what they give you: a tote bag, a hat. Maybe a cheap watch. Crap. That's all. Real crap.

But this… This is a TV. A miniature TV. The screen's only an inch wide. To tell you the truth, I don't know if I'll ever use it. My eyes aren't that good. Never were. Not that the rest of me's so great either. I'm a mess: emphysema, varicose veins. Constipation. I'm all clogged up, if you want to know. Nothing goes through.

I could sell it. The TV. Or maybe give it to my niece. She likes it when I give her things. In fact, I think that's the only time she's happy to see me. When I've got something for her. Otherwise, she ignores me. What the hell. I wasn't any better as a kid. Kids are ungrateful, and that's the plain truth. Just as glad I don't have any.

But I think I'll keep it. Just so people can see. So they can ask, "What's that?", and I can tell them, "I won it. Everybody in the bank wanted it, but I'm the one who got it. Me." Maybe they won't understand why that's important. Maybe they already won some money in the lotto, or a set of Tupperware, or a trip. Or a car even. A friend of mine knew someone once. They won a whole car. You still have to pay the taxes, so it's not like it's completely free. But still, a whole car.

I say, good for them, if that's how it is. Good someone likes them, and I'll bet their health is good too. Most people get a little bit of luck anyway, even if it doesn't last. They get something, sometime. It's like a right, you know?

Not me. That's not how it is with me. This is something special for me. This is a first. 'Cause there's something I want you to know:

I ain't never won nothin' in my whole life.

Name in the Paper

This just ain't fair.

He did it, didn't he? Sure he did. Christ, he was holding the knife when they caught'm. Still had the blood on it, too.

On top of that, he confessed. Right off. Said he didn't need no lawyer. He knowed what he'd done and he didn't mind them knowin' it too.

Well, Dowdie always was two tracks short of a train. Never did love that boy for his brains.

Still, he did it, didn't he? And they wrote about it, too. Put it right there in the paper. The whole story. First boy I ever had made the news. Isn't that somethin'? There it was, clear as day: his name, and the name of our town too!

Oh yes, I was proud, let me tell you. Near to burstin'. Except for one thing. No picture! Can you beat that? He got'm an article, a whole entire paragraph. And no picture.

Well, I called up that newspaper, asked for the fella that wrote the thing. "I can bring you a picture," I says. "Got one right here. Only a few years old." 'Course he didn't have that scar back then. The one Al-John give'm with his hook? But what of it? It's him, ain't it? Why, of course it is.

Now at first, it's like he's a little surprised that I want'em to put Dowdies' picture in there. So I try to explain. "Look, Mister, wasn't any of my family ever got hisself in the papers. Not so much as a 'bituary. So naturally we're all terrible proud. Oh yes sir, we are. Only, don't you see, it'd be a whole lot better with his picture in there. Now, here's what you're gonna do: I'm gonna bring you this here picture, and tomorrow, you just go right ahead and print the whole thing all over again, only this time you'll have a picture."

Well then – do you know, it sounded like he was covering up the mouthpiece there for a moment –, but then he says, "I'm sorry, Ma'am, but I don't think we can do that."

"Now, why the Hell not?" I says. And then he starts goin' how there's all this news, and how it's different every day, and they just don't need to be puttin' in the same article all over again. And that was pretty much that.

Now I ask you, is that fair? I mean, if they'da done it right the first time. Even if they had to use one of them mud shots. You know, where they stick a number on you, and don't nobody ever smile?

Though, you know, Dowdie, he probably did smile. He probably smiled real big.

The Seven Dollar Special

Now, I want you to bring me a nice piece of chicken. And make sure that it's not too well done. Nice and tender's how I like it. You be sure to tell them. And I'll have the cup of paprika soup to start with. That is what it is today, the paprika or the vegetable? Well, then paprika it is.

You see? I'm not even Hungarian. But that's how long I've been coming here. Enough to prefer the paprika. And let me tell you, I made quite a face the first time I saw it. Yes indeed.

Hold your horses! I can see it's crowded. You always do get quite a crowd for lunch. And well you should. It's quite a bargain, this menu. But I see they have the strudel today. I don't want the strudel. I'd like the apricot crepe. Don't look so sour, young man. I've been coming here since before you ever saw this country. Since I worked at that milliner's up the block. I know perfectly well what it says on the menu. But you just tell them it's for Mary, and they'll be happy to make the change. Oh, I'm sure they will.

Do you know, I remember when this was the three dollar special? That's right, three dollars for all of it: the starter, the main plate, the dessert. And that little dish of beet salad they used to give you. That wasn't even on the menu, but you always got it. That was nice. To get a little extra they didn't even have to give you.

Well, what you can do? Everything's more expensive now. I suppose they had to cut corners somewhere. And it's still enough to fill me up. It'll have to, won't it? It'll have to tide me over until tea and toast tonight. You wait until you have to live on a pension, young man. It's no picnic, let me tell you.

Oh go on then. Go wait on the other customers. Laszlo – that was the old man's name who died, wasn't it? – well, Laszlo, he always had a little time to talk. But you don't even understand half of what I'm saying, do you?

Now you be sure to tell them about the chicken. Nice and tender. And don't forget the crepe. Tell them Mary doesn't want the strudel, she wants the crepe. I'm sure they'll be happy to make the change.

Kiss-Kiss

Yes. Well, of course. Absolutely.

Well, I wouldn't mind. No, not one bit. Though it would depend.
Oh yes, it would. It would certainly depend.

Not that I'm doubting. My goodness, no! Not for a minute.
Please, please, you mustn't think that. Why I – What? Oh well, I
can see where it might sound like that. Misunderstandings do
happen. Isn't that so? – Why of course they do. Really regrettable.
That's just how it is. – I said, that's just how it is. Well, it is. Oh
yes. Yes, I'm quite convinced. 100%. – Do you, now? Do you? I
see. Yes. Well, of course, that's your point of view. – No, not for a
minute. I'm sure you have your reasons. – Well, your reasons for –
I didn't say you were wrong. I most certainly did not. No, no, I did
NOT. What I said was – Well, if you'll just listen to me for a
minute. Yes, a minute. – Excuse me? No I do NOT think I talk a
great deal. Why, as it happens, now that you should bring this
subject up – No, not long-winded, exactly, just... a breath now and
then. That's all. I'm suggesting. Some room for another person's –
Not that I mind. Mind! Good Lord, no! Why, we're friends, aren't
we? Have been for years. No one I care for more. Honestly.
Scout's honor. Yes, yes. Cross my heart and hope to die. Honestly.
– Love you too.

Well then. See you tomorrow. – Promise. Double triple promise.
Kiss-kiss!

Denture Daddy

Stop looking at that girl, Howard. That one's too young for your grandson.

There's not enough Viagra in the world, honey. Not to get your old bones in that saddle. You just take that heartbeat down before you hurt yourself.

I know, Sweetie. Once upon a time. Once upon a time, you would have gotten on your charger and STORMED that castle. Or played sweet music until she dropped her drawbridge.

Of course, you would have, Sweetie. It was just like that. I'm sure you remember every detail.

Oh for Gods sakes, stop playing with your teeth. You're going to lose them again. It's not like we can afford to keep buying you a new set. I'm telling you, it's back to baby food if that happens again. And for a lot longer than a month this time.

Though you did like the banana purée. Couldn't get enough of that, now could you?

Well, that can be arranged. Drop those choppers again and you'll start to think those little jars are Cordon Bleu.

So what do you say, Honey? Are you up to the walker or should we ask for some wheels? Either way, it's a long trek back to the barnyard. We'd better give ourselves some time.

It's not like we can count on getting any from anyone else, now can we?

The Cut-Rate Job

Poor Tomas. Did you see his wife? They did a lousy job, huh? You can hardly recognize her. It looks her cheeks are falling off her face.

That one guy, the neighbor? He came in and he started to walk right out. He's thinking, "Did I come to the right funeral?" And he'd been living right next to her! Saw her everyday!

But can you blame him? She looks like she's melting up there. It's like they took out all her bones. Who could ever tell it was her?

I think someone should say something to Tomas. He might not even realize it, all upset and all like he is. He may think that that's how she's supposed to look. You know, being that she's dead and all. He doesn't know. All he knows is, she's not there anymore. He probably isn't paying any attention to how she looks. Just like when she was alive, right? He probably doesn't even know that they could have made her look better. That they could have made her look really nice. Not that she was ever what you'd call pretty, but you know. Put a little tissue inside her cheeks, to maybe hold them up. Maybe add a little rouge on top of all that powder. Why shouldn't she look a little nice? Just because she's poor? They still could've made an effort.

It's not like he didn't pay them anything. They took his money, didn't they? OK, so maybe it wasn't the deluxe version. Maybe it's more like the Denny's version. But still, you know, you go to that Denny's, they give you a good meal. Nothing fancy, but they do it right.

Whoever did her, I don't even think he was paying attention. He was probably watching the ball game the whole time. And all he was worried about was, who was gonna score? He probably was hardly even looking at her. How could he have been? How could he'a been looking at her and left her like that?

I'm gonna say something to Tomas. Well, don't you think I should?

After the Storm

The weather's so incredible! I just love weather like this! Especially after all this gloom. It's simply been terrible. Awful. And I try to sympathize. You don't want to be insensitive. But, Good Lord, how long can this last? Things will look up! I don't doubt that for a moment!

But what do you do when you're surrounded by all these Cheerless Charlies, faces down, frowning, slumping, hardly standing upright, some of them.

Where does that get you? Tell me. How much mileage is there in that jalopy? You want to get your head up, square your shoulders and, by God, put one foot in front of the other. No matter how bad it gets. No matter how foul the clouds. No matter how dark the road.

And it has been dark. Oh yes it has. As if I didn't know that. As if I haven't felt the same pain. I've been there too, the whole time. Indeed I have. Right through the whole thing. But enough's enough, I say. It's time to shake a leg.

God, it truly is a glorious day!

The Lady of the Loading Dock

But don't you want to keep them for yourself? Why then, yes, I'd love to have them. They look simply delicious.

Thank you so much. That's very kind.

Is there something else? Something I could do for you? You look so…

Why, you're concerned about me, aren't you? Concerned how I get by out here. Now, don't you give it a moment's thought. Those nice men in the store tell me they don't use this loading dock anymore and they've been glad to let me stay here, as snug as you please. As you can see, I have my sleeping bag and my little valise, and that radio. That's a blessing, I must say. I can get all the classical stations, you know. And I do love my Bach. I played piano as a girl. Twelve years. Haven't touched one for ages, but do you know, when it's something I used to play, my fingers follow along with no trouble at all. Just like that. Just like it was yesterday.

There's one Mexican boy who brings me batteries. He calls me "*abuela*". Isn't that sweet? That means "grandmother" in their language. Anyway, I don't really need them. I haven't the heart to tell him. They let me plug it in, right there in that post.

It would be nice to have a bathroom more than once and again, I must say. I used to be a very tidy person, you know. Quite fastidious about my person. But then, some things can't be helped, can they?

Still, you see, you mustn't worry about me. Not one little bit. I get along quite nicely, as you see.

And I do thank you for the crackers. Cheese and peanut butter, are they? My, how I will enjoy those. Oh yes, you can be sure I will. Why I'll gobble them up, every bite!

A Mused

A muse! Could anything be more tiresome?

He insisted that I be pure. That is, inaccessible. "Suit yourself," I thought. It's not like there weren't plenty of others.

Not that I wasn't selective. Don't misunderstand me. I required brilliance! I required ambition! I wanted some hint in the sweat and stink, in the coarse, crude grunting, of genius, of something finer than us both.

Call it an affectation. Some want diamonds, or the best champagne. I loved the image of my lover's name inscribed in stone, or printed in bold in an encyclopedia entry.

I found that quite erotic, really. Quite the aphrodisiac in its way.

Oh, I liked the others too, the Apollos and Adonis's, the bodies and the profiles nearly marble in their perfection. Marble-ous, you might say. But only for diversion. Only to remind myself that, if I really wanted to, I could. But those were naughty pleasures, like the hot dog you might grab on the street before dining that evening in a five star restaurant.

But you see? I didn't even demand virility. I didn't even demand, strictly speaking, that they have balls. Only talent. It only took talent to turn me on.

And yet... He preferred me virginal. A goddess beyond compare. And he got some excellent things out of it. Nothing to do with me, really. Just a few useful details. The mention of my name. But none of the flesh and blood, none of the urgent heat of my own breath.

Still, if it gave him what he wanted, and me a minor reputation, well, that's just fine, now isn't it?

As I say, from a strictly practical point of view, there were always lots of others.

Cell Walls

If you look very clearly, you can see the cell wall. The nucleus is easier, of course, like a little sun in that mini-cosmos. But it's the wall that defines the cell. The individual. And yet, you know, it's not very interesting. The nucleus is where the action is. Where it all happens.

I was hurt, yes, when my paper was rejected. I knew I was right, even back then. Thirty years ago. That's when I should have won this. And yes, I suppose I was a little hurt. But I didn't dwell on it at the time. The work itself was so involving. Prizes, tenure, all that – perhaps it should have mattered more. But I was always able to do my research. Which I haven't been lately. Not since the Prize. I seem to spend all my time talking to people like you.

Oh no! Please don't take that the wrong way! I'm terribly tactless, I'm afraid. Too many years spent out of the swim. Just me and my microscope, most of the time. Not the best place to hone your social skills.

Marriage? People always ask that. If I were a man, would it seem so strange to be married to my work? I suppose your paper will put it that way: "Married to her work."

Funny when you think of it. When a cell needs company, it simply divides in two. All it needs is itself. Maybe I've spent too much time with something that doesn't need others of its own kind.

A lot of the people who've come seem to find me very alone. As if I lived locked in this claustrophobic space. But that's the thing about this work. You forget about yourself.

That's the best part. You forget about yourself.

Little Attentions [full solo piece]

A LIVING ROOM WELL-FURNISHED IN A SOMEWHAT OLD FASHIONED STYLE: A CLAW-FOOTED COUCH, EASY CHAIRS AND HASSOCKS, A COFFEE TABLE. THE ONLY MODERN TOUCH IS A PC SET ON A SEMI-CIRCULAR WALL TABLE. THERE IS A WALL SWITCH RIGHT BEHIND IT.

AZALEE, A GREY-HAIRED WOMAN IN A DARK DRESS WITH A FLOWERED PRINT, IS STANDING IN FRONT OF THE COMPUTER. SHE ADDRESSES AN INVISIBLE INTERVIEWER BEHIND THE CAMERA.

AZALEE

Oh, I don't now if you'd call it a chat group, really. Aren't those with a bunch of people? This is just Howard and myself. That's right, just the two of us. And I don't really `log-in', as you say. My little friend here just beeps whenever there's a message.

BEEP

Well, there you are! Just like that. Whenever Howard sends me a message. Let's see what this one's about.

READS

Now, why does he do that? He knows it's too early for his next beer.

TYPES REPLY

Really! Just because he can't see me, he thinks I'm a soft touch! Well, he's got a lot to learn, now hasn't he? There now, what was I saying?

Oh yes. When there's a message, Pozzo here – that's what I call my little friend, Pozzo – Pozzo gives his little toot and if I'm not too busy, you understand, I come right over.

I do like that part, you know, that I can decide if I feel like it, and not have the old fool pestering me over and over again. When he was up here, that's how it was, all the time: "Azalee, bring me a beer!"; "Azalee, where's my paper?", "Azalee, could you bring me my teeth?'" – And try to ignore him, too, you just try!

BEEP

Oh, my heavens, what is it now?

READS

Oh yes! The ventilation. Dear me, I forgot all about that. It was only supposed to be off for a minute or so.

FLICKS ON THE WALL SWITCH

My, it must have been getting a little stuffy down there. Yes indeed!

BEEP – SHE READS

Well, of course, you ninny! The air won't just start rushing in all at once! You have to give it a few minutes!

You can see for yourself, can't you, how demanding he is? But maybe you're thinking, "Well, at least he's a lively one. Must be good fun to have around." Not a bit of it. Why, Pozzo here's better company, most of the time.

BEEP

What! Again? My, but he's frisky today! It's almost as if he knows you're here.

READS

Well, no, Howard, you can NOT have a beer yet. No is no, and that is that.

You know, I am SO glad I don't have to listen to that voice of his. That's what's so wonderful about Pozzo. I thought at first we'd have to have an intercom. Now that would have been excruciating.

Anyway, he doesn't know you're here, of course. Hasn't the foggiest idea what goes on anywhere else. Unless it's on a football field. Not that that's such a change. He wasn't the fastest dog running, even when he was sitting here, right in that chair.

Now there are women who get very upset, who've been known to put a little something in the pot roast, if you know what I mean. Or get out that hunting gear hubby's kept so well-oiled all the while he was ignoring her needs. But personally, I just don't think violence is the answer. Though I don't imagine there's a gal of any age who didn't applaud that Bobbit girl just the teensiest bit. Poor thing.

BEEP – SHE READS

Oh, for goodness sake. Another B.M. This from a man who was constipated a month running, more often than not. Put the bucket on the hook, you big baby. I'll bring it up when I'm ready.

TYPES, CLICKS

Anyway, I just had the basement modified a little – Howard never noticed, he always said fixing up the house was my department – and then when everything was ready, well, it did take some doing getting him down there, I'll admit that, but when he came to and there it all was, the TV and his crossword, and his first few rations of beer, oh, I imagine he got used to it pretty quickly. At least he hasn't been complaining all that much. Not since the first week.

BEEP – SHE READS

Oh, for goodness sake. Well, I suppose I'd better go and get him one of his silly beers. I know, I shouldn't indulge him like this. But really, you young people could learn a thing or two from the likes of us. It's these little attentions that make a marriage last.

MATURE: Male

Teacher of the Year

No doubt, as you embark upon this next stage in your great journey of learning, you are asking yourselves, "Why?"

"Why sixth grade?"

Ah yes! Why indeed? Far be it from me, a humble priest in the Temple of Enlightenment, whose salary may be less than that of your paperboy and is certainly less than those of those coverall-clad Neanderthals who clean these very corridors – far be it from me, I say, to decipher so deep a mystery.

For still fresh in your young minds, I fear, is the traumatic betrayal inflicted in *fifth* grade – an ordeal most of you will have endured under the disastrous tutelage of Mr. Bellmop, my former schoolmate, as it happens, and now for too long a colleague. So blasted will the sunlit peaks of your youth have been by the fumblings of this incompetent, you now face what should be the most glorious perspectives with, it is safe to say, raw terror.

Blindly led astray as you have been, hopelessly unformed as your young minds are, what, what I ask you, am I possibly to do? Who can blame me for simply throwing up my arms at the prospect and, well, to put it plainly, giving up?

I mean, let's face it, you don't have a prayer, most of you. You might as well just go back to fourth grade, start all over again, and hope old Snotfinger – oh yes, that's what we called him back in the schoolyard, bet he didn't teach you *that*, did he? That's right, "Snotfinger", I'll leave it to you to imagine why – well, you just hope that old Snotfinger Bellmop, Mr. Teacher of the Year, five years running, well, you just hope he's finally been revealed as the fraud he is and, before he can get you back in his clutches, unceremoniously shown the door!

So, that's my proposition. Just give it some thought, why don't you? And in the mean time while you're, each and every one of you, working out how to break the awful news to Mom and Dad, well, let's all just have a little nappy, why don't we? You'd like that, a little nappy-bye, wouldn't you?

Fine. Suit yourselves. Those who don't want to put their angelic little heads down can just teach each other where babies come from or compare notes on your parents' most intimate habits.

Just keep it down, won't you?

Oh, and that 'Snotfinger' thing? That's just between us, OK? If you value your goldfish, that is.

Bagel

If they had any brains, they'd be dangerous.

Lemme spread this cream cheese on my bagel. Only got a fifteen minute break. Not that the Mau-Mau would say anything. But she lets me know it. You can bet on that. Even when I'm back a minute early. "Oh Carl, honey, I came looking for you. I guess you were off having that late breakfast of yours."

Damn right. Same late breakfast I've had for thirty years. It's not like I have time when I leave the house. It's a long ride down from Yonkers. I'm not so young anymore. I need my sleep. But even back then, back when a boss looked like you and me, no tits, no attitude, no… tan, well, it's just a little habit I got into, and what of it? I know my stuff. I put in a good day, starting at eight, straight through 'til five. I earn my pay. Every measly cent. They're lucky to have me. Not that they know it. It's *me* should be watching *her* breaks. Waddya want? Affirmative action. Bank's afraid of gettin' sued. So they put the Mau-Mau in charge. A woman, too. Wow. A double-header. That really looks good in a full-page ad. Don't know how they fit that caboose of hers on the page though.

Anyway, tell you the truth, I'm glad not to have the job. Who needs the headache? Lots of late hours, doing budgets, going to meetings. Bunch'a crap. Rather just punch my code. We used to really do that, you know. Really. It was all on cards. You wanted to fix a call, you punched a hole. Honest. Then you'd wait three days for the job to run. One bug and back to work. Had to wait for days just to see if the fix worked. You got careful, back then, lemme tell you. You did it right. Not like it is today.

But what is, right? You did your work back then, it counted for something. You got your credit, you got your grade. It wasn't all about politics, all this equal opportunity crap. You could smoke at your desk, instead of sneaking out in the goddamn cold. Talk about unhealthy. Pneumonia's unhealthy. You could tell a joke that was a little risqué. Or maybe not about a white person. The colored weren't so touchy. What there were of them. Hell, we'd tell them the same jokes we told everybody else. And they'd laugh too. Never said boo. Not until someone told 'em to, that is.

Hell, now they're putting them in charge and they're still complaining. Complain even louder now that they got what they want. Isn't that always the way?

Aw, what the hell, soon it won't be my problem. I'll collect my pension and this place can kiss my ass. If the cholesterol don't get me first. Got this young doctor, tells me to cut out the cream cheese on my bagel. Can you imagine that?

They don't wanna leave us nothing, I'm tellin' you. They just want to take it all away.

Scrivo, Ergo Sum

I've written a number of books. Oh, none are published. Too advanced. You can't expect publishers to understand. They're store keeps, really. They should be made to stand behind counters, wearing big white aprons. Like butchers. "Yes, sir, which cut of the market would you like today/ A thriller? A self-help book? A scandalous biography? What? You don't want something from the market? You don't want a cut of the usual fare? Why that... that's preposterous! Original? Original work, did you say? Please. Do we look like we serve literature here? Do we look like we serve culture? I'm sorry, my friend, but you're in the wrong place. I really must ask you to leave. Move along now, won't you? Move along and there won't be any trouble."

Perfectly clear then, isn't it? Why none of them want my books. No interest at all. Not a nibble. What does it matter to them, my years of research, my penetrating insights, my entirely unique perspective? Perfectly worthless, don't you see? Not worth a *sou*! Not the most pitiful part of a *centime*.

No, I am condemned to labor in the utmost obscurity, a candle unto myself, a discreetly disreputable entity., disturbing enough were I to be observed, but perfectly harmless as things stand. And so I scribble, yes I scribble, cover innocent unblemished sheets of paper, disfigure and deface their curious purity, blast across their ivory the fine sharp streams of my rage.

Wilbur

I'm bored.

I've been sitting here firing people all day. On paper that is. None of them have been told. I don't do that part. That's what Wilbur's for. Maybe later I'll fire Wilbur. But not until he's told them. Oh no.

It's hard work, this. Someone's got to run the company. Preferably not me. Not day to day, anyway. Wilbur does a lot of it. But he'll need a few people to help. Unless I fire him. Then I'll have to pick one of them. One of the leftovers. Which means I'll have to learn something about them.

Now that will really be boring.

This was fun at first. It's an art, you know. The highest salaries have to go. But you don't want to end up with incompetents either. Which means you dump some of the cheap ones too. Because if they never went anywhere, they're can't be that good.

What you really want is the worker bees. The ones who bust their rear ends hoping to get up another notch. The ones who get way up there are too busy playing politics and sticking their snouts up Wilbur's seat. Or up mine, if I make it available. Which I only do at choice moments. Can't let them get too used to top quality.

It's not that they're downright incompetent. Just that they've spent all their time apple-polishing, so that usually they've lost their touch for the nuts and bolts.

Which means I don't need most of them. But one or two I do. And maybe Wilbur. Wilbur knows my wants. That's not a talent to scoff at. On the other hand, it gives him more power than he should really have.

So I'll have to think about Wilbur. I'll really have to think about Wilbur.

But all the other names? The ones on the list? I'm really, really sick of looking at them. I'll be damn glad when they're gone.

Then maybe, and with Wilbur to think about, well then maybe I won't be so bored.

The Festival

I'd stopped for the night on my way down. With less than no expectations. Meal and a roof for the night. Just have a quick drink after, and be off to bed.

She was sitting at the bar. A beauty. Say twenty-five. Nothing flashy, but even in slacks and a simple top, a tall bit of all right, you know?

"What the hell?" I thought.. "I'm not dead yet. I can look."

"Had a fight with my husband," she said. "He took off. My neighbor's got the kids. I just needed to get out. Clear my mind."

Needed to talk. That's fine. I'll listen. I enjoyed it actually. It's not like we had much in common. Even when I was her age, I was in the thick of things, going for the gold. People like her don't stray too far from what they know. But she was no fool, either. And nice to look at. Oh yes, that she was.

Half an hour into this, she asks me, "Do you want to go dancing?" Well, why not. Why not's the right answer when a beautiful woman invites you for a whirl.

The club was right next door. And, do you know, it was OK. Just what it was. Not trying to be more, you know? But the music was good. And I got to hold her close. Now that was nice. She felt like she looked. A warm one. Sweet.

We got up quite a sweat, as it worked out. And I dropped a few years along the way.

Then she said, out of the blue, "You know, I really don't want to be alone tonight. Can I come stay with you?"

Ah. Well, now, I knew where this was going. But what the hell. A few extra bucks for a good time. Hell, I can certainly afford it. And it wasn't a bad way to end the night.

Ah, the night. There's things that can't be put into words. They really can't. No complaints, is all I can say. No complaints at all.

She woke me up early and said, "I'd better get back. My kids'll be wondering where I am." Myself, I was in no hurry to arise, but, I told myself, there are things that must be done. Business is business after all.

I reached for my pants and took out my wallet.

Well, let me tell you, her mouth fell wide open. "Oh my God, did you think –? I wasn't doing this for *money*. I just wanted some company."

Lucky for me, she didn't take offense. One quick kiss and off she went. Leaving, I must say, a very happy me.

Can you beat that? Beautiful young girl like that? And me the age I am?

So, I've got some deals working here. Promising, too. But however the festival goes, let me tell you. This has already been a good trip. This has been a *damn* good trip!

Hands

My hands aren't what they used to be. They don't move as well. They don't feel with the same intensity. Even to look at... Well, they've got character, I suppose.

I look at the work and I wonder, "How did I make that? How did my muscles know to move that way? How did they change tension and intent so exquisitely? How did they gain and surrender strength as the moment demanded, expanding, contracting, moving rapidly, moving almost not at all? All in service of this image. All in simple echo of my mind.

I had mastery of them then. Which is to say, I was unaware of them at all. They simply responded. We had our mission, our urge. After my studies, after that early discipline, after those hours and hours of practice, they were like my voice, my sight. More sense than instrument. An emanation of myself. As if I was merely the conduit of a vision.

Ah, how wonderful not to have to think! Not to have to struggle! To only, in those moments, *be.*

And all through my hands. The same hands I eat with, climb with, clean with. These vulgar, functional tools. My paws, my pincers, my claws. My tentacles and suckers, that might in another life have tugged me along the ocean floor. My pseudopods.

It's wonderful what they were to me. It really is. I suppose I must forgive them now. Forgive them for betraying me.

The Last Room

This is it. This is my room. It's not too bad. I've got a hot plate, and a microwave, and the mini-fridge. And the TV. That was my big splurge. But it was worth it. It's my window on the world. Hell. I'm here almost all the time. Might as well have a nice window, no?

Oh I go out for walks. I've still got my health, knock on wood. And there's the little errands, groceries, mostly, dry cleaners once a month. Laundry's right here in the building, so I don't have to go far for that.

But most of the time, I'm right here. And most of that, I spend in front of the TV. Right in front of the TV, as you can see. About three feet away. It's not like I've got that much room. Don't know if it's good for my eyes, sitting so close.

What the hell, if they haven't given out by now.

Otherwise, I just sit on the edge of my bed mostly, and look through old pictures. My Navy days, a few trips with my wife. Old albums of family pictures. Some go pretty far back; Civil War, about. I don't know who'll get them after I'm gone. My brother had a heart attack a few years back. Neither of us had any kids. So there's just me now.

To tell you the truth, though, I'm in pretty good shape. So I could be around for a while. Maybe another twenty years. Hell, thirty, the way they fix you up these days. And do you know, chances arc, I'll spend them all right here, right here in this room, right in front of this very same TV.

Hell of a thing to look forward to, isn't it?

The Cornerstone

It would seem I'm going to die. If I'm to believe the doctors. And I've always been inclined to. Even now. Even when it would be tempting to doubt them.

But that's not how I've brought you up, is it? To rail and rant at unwelcome truths. Keats was right, you know, in that ode of his:

> *When old age shall this generation waste,*
> >   *Thou shalt remain, in midst of other woe*
> *Than ours, a friend to man, to whom thou say'st,*
> >   *"Beauty is truth, truth beauty"*

And so it is. Even the harshest truth has a kind of beauty, just as the most well-intentioned deception turns out ugly, as often as not.

I've told you all this before, though, haven't I? I must have, somewhere in all these years. We only have so many ideas, most of us. Much as I tried to keep mine fresh. Anyway, I hope you'll allow me that one small homage to age, to repeat myself a little.

But I'm avoiding the subject, aren't I? Despite myself. And I tried so hard to speak it plain. After all, what could be plainer? It's as plain as a stone. A large white stone. Cut it and carve it as you will, there it is: a stone. In front of us both.

We'll have to make it a cornerstone now, though, won't we? The cornerstone on which you and I will build what's left of my days.

ADULT: General

Vampire

Are you using your life? Your whole life? Do you mind if I borrow a bit of it?

I'll try not to be greedy. I may just take a memory. Or an anecdote. Or maybe a moment you didn't even notice. You wouldn't mind that, would you? Why you barely paid attention when it happened.

But I noticed. Oh yes. And it piqued my appetite right away. I wanted it, then and there. I wanted to taste it. I wanted to take it in. I wanted to digest it, to make it part of me.

That's how I live, you know. Off bits and scraps of other people's lives. I'm not too greedy, generally. Only once in a while will I take a whole hope, or a love affair, or that one family secret you'd worked so hard to keep. And a whole life? All the years and fears and ups and downs, and sickening, soul-crushing defeats and stirring, succulent victories?

Why, hardly ever. From time to time. When appetite... well, appetite just overcomes me.

Sorry...

I'm sorry. I really am. Sometimes, I just can't help myself.

But normally, just a nibble, a morsel, a little snack to tide me over. That's all. Not much. Nothing substantial.

Is that so bad? Do you really mind?

Yes, yes, I know. It's your life. But let's be honest: you weren't doing much with it yourself, now were you?

Purple

What, are you waiting for it to turn purple? There's only three colors, pal: red, green and yellow. It just turned green. If you don't move your damn car, it's gonna turn yellow. And you know what comes after that? Red! And you know what that means? We get to sit here. That's right! We get to sit here and do it all over again!

OK. That's it. Stop talking to whichever friend of yours is holding up traffic at some OTHER intersection and start moving. What the – Oh no. Well, sure if you give the pedestrians time to get into the crosswalk, they're going to grab their chance. That's why we don't want to wait, see? That's why the moment it turns green, we put our friend on hold and we MOVE.

Oh no! Oh dear God no! See? That's the second color. That's yellow. And you don't have to worry about it, cause you're already in the intersection. But if it turns red –

Like that, for instance. Like it just did. Oh dear God.

Bye. Have a nice trip. Nice being stuck in traffic with you while you forget how to drive.

But don't worry. I'll be thinking of you. With this red light? Hell, I'll be thinking of you for a long time.

Local Color

Ah, don't believe what you hear.

Sure it used to be a colorful neighborhood. That old diner that's boarded up now; Jumping Jack's Deep-Fried Franks; this one bar where the guys went when they got out of lock-up. Or that pool hall where hookers would hand you the cues. Yeah, it had atmosphere. Flavor. Funk. Whatever.

But it wasn't like you actually wanted to live there. Please. You could smell the pee in the doorways. Cat stink in the alleys. And the food? Well, those hand-painted signs sure looked picturesque. But one glance at the grill, with the grease gathered up at the back like sooty snot, and you had to be seriously drunk or dying of hunger to chow down at the diner. How about Jumping Jack's, with the big polka dot clown up top? That stand stank of sizzling fat. Not to mention the franks looked like something off a mummy's crotch. The sign would sell you, the food would fell you.

Sure, it was a sad day when they tore it all down. And they haven't put much up so far but concrete walls and a chain link fence. But believe me, that's all that could make what used to be here beautiful. 'Cause the truth is, it never was that great.

The Egyptians Had a Word for It

Now, this isn't some kind of pyramid scheme. I want to be clear about that. We've got a product here. Good product. Can't keep up with the demand. Very good product.

What I'm saying is, it's an opportunity. You're letting others in on something big. They're going to want to thank you. They're going to be that grateful.

And they're not the only ones. Not the only ones at all. Because you get to share. You get to share your good luck. With your neighbors, old friends, family members. Anyone you care about. You can include them in.

And here's the best part: in helping them, you're helping yourself. That's right. Because every hundred they make, you make ten percent of that. That's good, right? You don't mind ten percent, do you? Think of that. Sign on ten people and you make the whole hundred. That's all it takes. Ten. You've got ten friends, right? You can do that in no time, now can't you?

Me, I get a percentage too. And I won't lie to you. It is a little larger. Once you're an associate VP, you get a bigger cut. That's only fair. That's just reason, now isn't it? Of course it is. You see my point. I knew you would.

'Cause you're sharp. Not everybody gets it. You'd be surprised. But you do. Because you're smart. So you get it. I can see that. I like that.

Now, figure each one of them signs up ten people, then that's when you start to see the serious money. Cause that's when you get to apply to be an AVP. Of course, there's an investment up front. That's just logical, right?

But not only are you getting the 10%, now you're getting your bigger slice, because probably you're an AVP. Well, I say probably, yeah, because, when you pay the fee, what you're doing is, you're applying, you see? It's not like a guarantee, you know? Because they have to be sure you're qualified. That's right, isn't it? That's only fair.

So, let's just think positive, you're an AVP, you've got a hundred people working for you, then they each get ten people – that's easy, right? Friends, colleagues, neighbors, anyone can get ten in no time. Then you've got a thousand. A thousand people and you're getting a cut from everyone. Think about that. You're not even WORKING anymore and you're getting a cut from all these people.

I'm telling you, it's fantastic. It's a fantastic product. It really is.

Gone Cat

That cat could blow sackbut six ways to Sunday. None of that noodling up and down the scales. Straight ahead, with a horn full of statement. His guts in the changes and his foot on the beat. Say what you will, he was never halfway. He was always one hundred percent.

The ladies liked that. You know they did. They'd play "Misty" for him in their undies. Sashay past the stage with their stuff up, hoping and praying that he'd look down. And I guess he must have, somewhere on the side of his climb, of his careful creep and slide up that tune. Because he found them later, once the sound shut down and he was off the ride, walking among us mortals. He'd find one of them most nights, find her as sure as a bat finds a moth, at least long enough to break her heart.

Did I happen to mention I hated his guts? Oh yeah. He was a bastard and a half. He'd spit poison into Paradise and smile to see the trees turn brown. He'd shoot down your sweetest dream and hope you got cut by the falling pieces.

How come he got the gift? I never have dug that. He should have been left in the mud, wriggling around with the other worms. But he was the ones the gods touched, and gave a hand up to Heaven. And the rest of us? Well, we got to stare up from the dust and watch him fly.

Ashes

Just move that if it's in your way. I should really find some other place to put it.

What it is, it's my father's ashes.

I've had them awhile now. He died about twenty years ago. Yeah.

We meant to bury him. At the time. It's just... Well, it was messy. At the time. And we never got around to it.

I should do that. We should do it, that is. Me and my sibs. We've talked about it. Yeah. We have. It's just... well, things come up. And it's not like we get together all that much. We've all gone our separate ways.

I'm not sure how I ended up with them. I've offered to let one of the others take them. But they just say, "No, no, that's fine. No, you hold on to them."

So I do. It's not like they're in the way. Well, except for now of course. But like I said, it's fine if you move them.

It's just something that's there, you know, and you get used to it, and you know you should think about it, do something about it, but after a while, a long time goes by, and you still haven't. And it's still there.

Twenty years later, it's still there.

Chicken

This is how shattered we were:

We had bought a chicken. We'd been sitting around the living room for three days. But finally, some of us got the strength to go shopping. And we bought the chicken. Not a whole one. Cut up in parts. But no one thought to put it away. So it sat there on the counter.

I stopped by it myself several times, staring at the shallow bubbles of blood oozing against the clear wrapping, pressed by the puckered skin. The skin was all yellow and white. Where it was torn, the pink muscle showed, sleek, plump, ending in white tendons which clung to a clean knob of bone. On one piece, bits of liver or kidney remained, bulbous brown drops speckling the membrane over the ribs.

I especially remember that organ meat, dotting the delicate bones.

After a few days, it started to rot. You had to be in the kitchen to smell it. But the odor there became overpowering, dense and sweet. The color didn't change. That curved, pink muscle looked perfectly fine. But the odor was unbearable. I remember hurrying in and hurrying out.

In the end, it must have gone beyond the kitchen. Maybe it reached us in the living room. Someone must have finally thrown it out. Perhaps it was even me.

Beat It

My heart's outside. That's the best way I can say it.

It beats OK. It beats hard. But not for me. I'm just watching. I'm not connected. My blood's a swamp. My pulse is dumb. I'm not hearing it. My heart's a happy thumper out there on its own. But I'm not invited. I'm watching it on the monitor, too bored to change the channel.

I wish I could say that I'm giving up. The truth is, that'd be too much effort. Too much of a decision. I'm not into commitment. And that's a big one. Giving up. Giving up completely. Oh no, it's not like I'm doing that.

I'm just a spectator, that's all. Pay per gloom. I get to sink at my own pace, while that big red heart out there, the one with all the energy, keeps on making all this fuss.

It's kind of amazing, don't you think? I think so. – Sucking blood in, pushing blood out Sucking blood in, pushing blood out... I find all that effort quite entertaining.

Though I may have to say something soon. I really may. Sometime in the next decade. I may just have to ask that beat to keep it down.

The Curve

Note, if you will, the careful curve, the sustained pressure with which the artist effortlessly defines a unique and particular form.

This rigor, so casually practiced, is typical of the work and appears even in the earliest student efforts.

It is all the more striking in light of the artist's life, which by any standard was chaotic and consistently free of any concern for order or clarity. Drug use and sexual debauchery do not in themselves imply disorder, but add to them his notorious disregard for hygiene and the legendary disarray of his innumerable residences, and the question becomes difficult to avoid: how did a life lived outside the most ordinary constraints give rise to a body of work which is a model of formal perfection?

The answer, we must presume, lay in a hunger, a hunger that nowhere else in this artist's life was ever fulfilled. Abandoned as a child, frequently homeless, subject to bouts of mental instability, he was unable ever to create, in his own life, anything like order. And yet he craved it. Craved it profoundly. And so, alone at his easel – in the midst of whatever catastrophic clutter may have surrounded it – he reached into his yearning and brought forth, this, this singular, pure harmony. He scrupulously, lovingly coaxed it onto the canvas – before abandoning himself to yet another orgy, another hellish descent into drugs or simple madness...

For a brief moment, with all his being, he struggled to give the rest of us what he never, in his short tortured life, was ever able to give himself.

Lake Dawn

You wake up by the water, and the sun cuts through the mist, and you can hear the birds, scattered in the shadows, one or two gliding against the sky. It's noisy in a way, but quiet too. Because everything fits together, and nothing's in a hurry.

It's a little cold, until the sun gets higher, and you have to be careful getting up, 'cause everything's wet. Glittering and pretty enough, but wet.

Still, it's worth getting up early and going outside. Just to take a deep breath, and stand there, and listen. Because it's that one moment when everything's waiting. When anything can happen. When the light throbs softly in the air. And if you really breathe it in, if you really really listen, well then, maybe you can keep it, just a little, maybe you can hold it in your hand, and maybe you can carry it, like fire, very quiet fire, all through the day.

Warning

It's taken me time to accept it. But it's true. You're an evil person, plain and simple. A profoundly bad person.

Maybe, if someone could ultimately work their way through that labyrinth to where the real, original you is hidden, maybe they'd find a reason, even for you. Did something happen to you, very, very early in Life? Maybe it's a matter of wiring, something chemical that happened before you were ever born. I don't know. Frankly, by now, I don't care. Because whatever the reason, however far back it goes, you're not going to change. You will try and hurt people every chance you get. You will destroy anything you can. Hell, even if it hurts you, you'll do it, as long as you can hurt someone else.

That's how much you like it. You like doing evil.

Now, before you give me some line about how you're misunderstood, let me be crystal clear. I don't care. I'm not your damned therapist. Luckily for you, I'm not even a cop. All I want to do is protect myself. And to protect those I love.

What I'm saying is, stay away from us. We don't want you here. We don't want you calling us. We don't want you in our lives. Period. And don't bother saying it isn't fair. That everything I've heard is lies. That you want another chance.

Just listen to what I'm saying, and take it seriously. Then stay the hell away.

Anchors

He thought no one would care. That he didn't matter. That's what's so hard.

How did I make him feel that way? I loved him so much. He was so much a part of my life. Even when I didn't see him. Sometimes I'd be struggling with an idea, and when it came out right, I'd think, "Why, that's exactly how he would –". And I'd wonder what he was doing, and think of calling him up. And then I'd get busy, and I wouldn't.

You always think people will be there. Like it's your right. Like someone gave you a guarantee. Fine, don't call them today, they'll be there tomorrow. Call them tomorrow.

How often do you think that they might be waiting for you to call? That they might need that reminder. That little signal that they matter. That little anchor that keeps them from drifting off.

How are you to know that they don't have enough of those just now, that there's this tide tugging them out and it's getting stronger and stronger, and there's less and less anchors of love, less and less, just when they need it most, just when they're letting go and floating away, there's less and less to hold them here, to hold them to Life?

Cold Cuts

Late that afternoon, Mrs. DiGiaccomo came over. She lived some miles down the road, and she'd known Dad pretty well. She was a large woman with doughy flesh hanging off her upper arms. When she hugged my mother, Mom looked like the child, though she was past fifty and Mrs. DiGiaccomo forty-nine.

Plus, with that big maternal hug, Mom started to cry. Again. Even though she didn't like her much. Mom thought she was low class.

She'd brought a platter of cold cuts: prosciutto, mortadella, provolone, interspersed with green and white pickles and black olives. It was covered with clear plastic, with a condolence card on top. One of those golden Italian things with too many angels. Mom glanced at the card and thanked her. To be polite, my half-brothers and I nibbled at the antipasti. For a few minutes, we did our best to talk. Then she got up, hugged Mom again, and left.

One by one, we began to pick at the brown and yellow spokes of food. Soon we were all bent forward around the platter, grabbing the greasy, rolled up meat and pale flaps of cheese. There was bread in the kitchen, but no one bothered to get it. Instead, we ate with our fingers, licking off the small bits of fat and pinching out the unground peppercorns, biting into pickled cauliflower and olives stuffed with shreds of pimento, gasping at the sharp spices and gulping in air as we swallowed the remnants of that wheel of food.

Soon there was nothing left but our chewing and smacking, our labored breathing, as we watched the Christmas lights flicker, staining the banks of snow.

Faith

I HAVE faith. That's what you must understand. I possess it. Yes, in a way, it possesses me. But at the same time, it is mine. In the same way as a lung, or a foot, or an ear. In the same way, I have life, I have faith.

Oh, I struggle. As some with failing sight struggle to see, to focus again; in the same way, sometimes my faith weakens, becomes indistinct. Not that faith is imperfect. But I am. Oh yes, I am.

Still, my faith remains mine, in weakness, in doubt, no less mine than any physical attribute or quality I have. Even more so.

You probe with your questions, you try – not very hard – to hide your pity, your sense that I am not quite right – as if this was a wig you could pull from me, as if it was a bubble you could prick.

And I welcome your probing, I welcome your assurance that I am blind, that I am lost. As a beach welcomes the water. As the water
welcomes the wind. Because your doubt is like a light on my conviction. Because it reminds me that what you want to chase away, this thing you want to cure me of, like a shadow across my vision, is bound with me like my blood. You can have it – I'd share it with you gladly – but you can never take it from me.

Stories

You know, that mousy little woman who mumbles when you greet her? The guy at the gate who just waves and smiles? That neighbor you've seen for years who never says hello.

They've each got a story. Each and every one of them.

Each one is a book. Maybe not an open book, but a book just the same. And no matter how plain the cover, none of those pages are empty. They're all packed with text.

Oh, sometimes you have to make a little extra effort. And other times you may not want to. You've got your own story, right? Maybe you don't have room for theirs. Or maybe, if you heard it, you'd wish you hadn't. Maybe you'd wished you'd left those covers closed.

I'm not saying you have to hear them all. In fact, you shouldn't. You'd go crazy if you tried. Long before you'd finished, you'd be babbling and drooling, trying to hold all these voices in your head.

All I'm saying is, know that they're there. That nobody is empty. Nobody has nothing to say. No matter how quiet, no matter how obscure.

Know that these stories are out there, just waiting to be told. Then choose a few, and tell them.

To order additional copies of this book

You can either go to the Chez Jim web site:

http://www.chezjim.com

or use the form on the following page. For further information, e-mail *jimchev@chezjim.com*

NOTE: Prices and availability subject to change. Please allow 4-6 weeks for delivery.

Complete this form and mail it with a check or money order (payable to *Chez Jim*) to:

Chez Jim, Box 103, North Hollywood, CA 91603

You may also want to confirm your order by e-mail (see above)

No. of copies	Notes	Cost
	@ $11.95 each =	
	CA residents add CA sales tax *8.25%:*	
	Add postage/handling:	
	$3.50 for first book	$3.50
	$1.00 for each additional:	
	TOTAL:	

PRINT MAILING ADDRESS:

Name

Address

City, State

ZIP

E-mail*

* Optional, for follow-up only. This and all other contact information is strictly for use by Chez Jim. We do not share this information with any other organization.

booksurge